The Forgotten Conscript

The Forgotten Chaldean

The Forgotten Conscript

A History of the Bevin Boys

by Warwick Taylor

First Edition 1995
The Pentland Press Ltd

Second Edition 2003
Warwick Taylor

Typeset and printed by
Babash Ltd
The Shadowline Building
Wembley Street
Gainsborough
DN21 2AJ

ISBN 1-904706-02-9

To my wife Sheila, without whose love and patience I should never have been able to research and write this book, which I have dedicated in recognition of all ex-Bevin Boys whether ballotees, optants or volunteers and to those miners who tolerated our presence.

Contents

List of Illustrations

Acknowledgements

Records
Public Record Office (All Crown Copyright material is
reproduced by kind permission of Her Majesty's Stationery
Office)
Bevin Boy Association
Big Pit Mining Museum
British Coal Corporation
British Library
Salford Mining Museum
Scottish Mining Museum
Yorkshire Mining Museum

Photographs
Beamish, The North of England Open Air Museum, County
Durham
Stuart Bicknell
British Coal Corporation
David Booth
John Cook
T. G. Fairbrother
Stanley Payne
Pontefract Museum
Salford Mining Museum
The Protector Lamp & Lighting Co. Ltd.
Denis Thorpe: *Manchester Guardian*
James Tuck

Drawings
Graham Grant

Miscellaneous Material
All the ex-Bevin Boys, too numerous to list.

Foreword

Fifty years ago, the arrival of the buff envelope explaining that their 'number had come up' changed the expectation and lives of many young men preparing to join the Services. The call applied to an entire cross-section of society. They were not allowed to say 'no'.

This book tells the tales about a largely unknown and almost forgotten army which played a key role in winning the Second World War - from far below the surface of the earth and in daily danger.

The Bevin Boys lived on site - mainly in hostels - worked underground and had difficulty in being released back into civilian life at the end of the war. They are still awaiting recognition, including having the Defence medal awarded - but live in hope.

This group is now meeting again on an annual basis. It is rare to find people whose age range is within three years of each other who have shared a life experience together and about which little is understood.

I was one of this group: I have my miner's hat and lamp to prove it - plus the happy memories of the ponies and friendships during my two and a half years in the pits (Notts and Derbyshire).

Lord Finsberg of Hampstead, M.B.E.
November 1994.

Introduction

Several books have been written by ex-Bevin Boys relating episodes of their own personal experiences in the coal mines, which is why I have deviated from this course. After several years of research, I have been able to gather information to enable me to reconstruct an authentic historical record of the Collieries, Training Centres, Miners' Hostels, Forms, Letters, Government and Parliamentary Debates of what went on behind the scenes during the wartime days of the nineteen forties.

It is intended to cover all aspects of those times and events, and will serve not only as a book of historical reference, but as a permanent record for those who took part, and for the generations that follow.

As this book is not intended to be a technical publication, details relating to surface and underground machinery have been kept to a brief general description. Terminology of equipment varied at collieries in the different Regions, but for purposes of description, the common general term has been used.

Some of the preserved records of facts and figures are either incomplete or limited in their information, and in order to avoid repetition, selection has been made from the most relevant detail for the years between 1944 and 1945 at the height of the Bevin Boy era.

Due to the large number of working collieries during the war, only photographs of the Training Centres and present day Mining Museums have been included. Wartime restrictions and unavailability of film has resulted in the shortage of photographs being available for that period and it has therefore been necessary to select suitable replacements taken throughout pre- and postwar years where little change had taken place. Unfortunately there are exceptions whereby, in spite of exhaustive research and enquiries, no photographs have been available of a particular training colliery or miners' hostel.

No official records of individuals have survived today, with the small exception of the Midlands Region.

It was generally thought that a Bevin Boy was placed into the coalmining industry because of his convictions as a conscientious objector. Facts show that there were only 41 out of a total of 47,859 Bevin Boys.

Warwick H. Taylor
Bevin Boy (Oakdale) South Wales

Rt. Hon. Ernest Bevin

*P.C. 1940; Lord Privy Seal since 1951; M.P. (Lab.) Central Wandsworth 1940-50.
East Woolwich since 1950; born 9 March 1881; married Florence Townley;
Member of MacMillan Commission on banking; member of Economic Advisory
Council, and of a number of other commissions and enquiries; National Organiser
of the Docker's Union. 1910-21; General Secretary of the Transport and General
Workers' Union, 1921—40; member of General Council of Trades Union Congress.
1925-40; Minister of Labour and National Service. 1940-45; Secretary of State for
Foreign Affairs, 1945-51, member of the Executive Committee of International
Transport Workers: Chairman Trades Union Congress, 1937; Hon. Fellow of
Magdalene College. Oxford. 1946; Hon. LL.D. Cambridge and Bristol Universities.
Publication: The Job to be Done, 1942 (speeches and broadcast addresses). Died
14 April 1951. (Who Was Who, 1951-1960.)*

Boy's Own Paper *(Yorkshire Mining Museum)*

1

The War Years

Shortly after the outbreak of World War II, a review of the unemployed on the coalmining registers, taken during the first six months of 1940, revealed that 17,000 were classified as fit to take up employment in coalmining, despite the fact that a further 23,000 were required to meet the labour needs of the industry.

By May the total number of persons on the colliery books was about 760,000 and the Mines Department estimated that an additional 40,000 workers would be required in order to raise output. Unfortunately a considerable number of coal miners had already left the industry to join other industries employed on war work with the attraction of higher pay and better working conditions. The loss of continental markets with the export of coal to Europe resulted in further unemployment, particularly affecting the Durham and South Wales coalfields. Between the September of 1940 and March 1941 a total of 15,359 in the Durham area and for a similar period for South Wales 21,000 unemployed colliery workers were being placed into other essential industries.

It was decided that an additional 40,000 workers were required and radio broadcasts were made appealing to ex-miners to return to the pits. Other difficulties were apparent but the needs of individual collieries were somewhat obscure, although there were in fact 34,000 unemployed attached to the industry.

The Mines Department and the Ministry of Labour sought ways of preventing workers from leaving the industry, by encouraging the return of suitable ex-miners from other industries as well as unemployed ex-miners and other suitable unemployed. As a means of solving the manpower problem, it was decided to make certain colliery workers at ages of eighteen, twenty-one, twenty-five and thirty the subject of a reserved occupation. Various schemes were put into operation between June 1940 and April 1942 to put a stop on enlistment in order to keep the numbers up in the industry. Additionally, twenty-two Tribunals were set up in seven areas for release of men for military service in an effort to see if young men could be called up into H.M. Forces, thus releasing other older unemployed miners back into the industry.

In March 1941 a decision was made that the control of labour forces would be more effective if an Essential Works Order was applied to the coalmining industry. However, problems arose over minimum wage agreements, Trade Union closed shop principles and the Miners' Federation wanting matters to be raised at National

Conference level, but in spite of this the Essential Works Order came into effect on 15 May.

By June the labour force in the industry had fallen to less than 691,000 and further radio appeals were made by the Ministry of Labour for the return of ex-miners, with the exception of those now employed in certain vital occupations. The appeal was disappointing and less than five hundred applications were received, although, as a result of appeals made during the previous year, ex-miners had started to filter back and by October a total of 509 out of 2,000 were found to be suitable for coalmining employment. Further regulations in force at the time compelled the registration of all ex-miners in July, with the result of 105,000 men registered of whom only 25,000 expressed their willingness to return to mining employment.

Previously it was decided that the industry was in need of 50,000 additional men and it was considered that the industry would obtain 35,000 men from registered ex-miners and that the Coal Production Council would not ask for the release of ex-miners serving in the Army. By November the labour force was approximately 707,000 but 720,000 would be needed to cope with coal production increases for the winter months.

The aim, already mentioned, was the return of 35,000 men, of whom 25,000 would be employed as face workers, back into the industry as quickly as possible. If this did not meet the requirements of the country in order to combat the coal shortage in the winter of 1941/42, then steps would have to be taken by the Government to release ex-miners from the army.

It was then realised that, with a manpower wastage at the rate of 28,000 a year, the figure would have to be increased to 40,000 in 1942. The effect of the return of more than 40,000 ex-miners had been disappointing. In the week ended 30 August 1941 a labour force of 700,608 produced an output of 3,998,700 tons, whereas in the following year, for the week ended 29 August, the output fell to 3,903,900 tons, although the labour force had been increased to 711,338.

In March 1942 it was decided to secure the immediate return to the mines of ex-coalface workers now engaged in other war industries. It was hoped that some 3,000 would be obtained from this source.

By June some 6,988 men had been interviewed and had been found suitable or potentially suitable. The reluctance of juveniles to seek employment into the industry was also notable, but in spite of the difficulties experienced in the transferring of men sent back into the mines from other industries, an additional 4,552 ex-miners had been returned to the pits between April and August, making a total of 38,309 sent back since the beginning of the campaign in the summer of 1941 and by

October the figure was 41,331.

The Government had already examined the question of reorganising the coal industry, by restriction of consumption (fuel rationing), measures for dealing with absenteeism, although this had already been established under the amended Essential Work (Coalmining Industry) Order 1942, which came into force in September.

This order was shortly amended to cover other issues of lateness, and indiscipline as well as absenteeism, whereby such offences could be prosecuted under Defence Regulations. The following April, new orders, consolidating previous orders which were revoked, now included provisions regarding working hours and dismissal for serious misconduct offences.

In June a Special Board of Investigation under the chairmanship of Lord Greene was set up recommending wage increases for underground and surface workers. This eventually led to a permanent conciliation machinery for negotiating wage scales and other matters within the industry, which was agreed in the March of 1943.

Figures estimated that some 82,000 men from the mining industry had joined the armed forces, but the number of ex-miners released by September 1942 were 7,915 from the army and 1,173 from the R.A.F., making a total of 9,088.

At the same time the Mining Optants scheme was introduced by the Ministry of Labour, whereby men under the age of twenty five when registering should be given the option to transfer to underground mining work as an alternative to serving in H.M. Forces. This measure only produced 2,750 men up to the end of June 1943, and it was found to be necessary to remove the twenty-five age limit altogether.

This option continued in force until the end of the European War, and the total number of men recruited by this method up to October 1945 was approximately 23,500.

Facts and figures taken from PRO: LAB 8/1473

2

Coalmining Ballot

In September 1943 the manpower situation in the industry was still giving cause for concern and an appeal was broadcast for 50,000 men and boys for work in the coalmines. Letters were sent to the Headmasters of Public and Secondary Schools asking for their co-operation to make potential school leavers aware of the situation. This was followed by a schools broadcast on 12 November, emphasizing the importance of coalmining to the war effort to pupils about to leave.

The response to the appeals was inadequate, and on 2 December 1943, the Rt. Hon. Ernest Bevin, Minister of Labour and National Service, made a statement in the House of Commons that was to change the lives of many thousands of young men aged between eighteen and twenty-five; on becoming available for call-up, they would be selected by ballot and thus conscripted into the coalmining industry as a compulsory alternative to service in the Armed Forces. The only exemptions to the scheme would be men in highly skilled occupations or already accepted for aircrew or submarine artificers.

The system of balloting would be by drawing one or more figures from 0 to 9 and those men whose National Service Registration Certificate numbers happened to end with the figure or figures thus drawn by ballot would be automatically transferred to coalmining. There was no question of choice; the Emergency Powers Act was in force and the Bevin Boy era was born.

The decision to take this drastic step was taken by the Government in an attempt to overcome the shortage of manpower in the industry: after the event, the value of the scheme was severely questioned. The difficulties in getting ex-miners back into the industry from the Services fell short of expectations and the Ministries of Fuel and Power, and Labour, had reached the end of their resources for bringing back ex-miners, and adopting fresh measures for attracting juveniles into the industry. After all, coalmining is dirty and hard work at all times and therefore, likely to remain unpopular in spite of improvements to working conditions, with the future possibilities of higher wages, shorter working hours, improved welfare and efforts to reduce industrial disease.

The ballot scheme was worked out during the autumn of 1943, and put to the Lord President's Committee on 19 November and then to the War Cabinet and out into effect in December. It was based on statistics in a paper put forward which stated that, since 26 September 1942, men under twenty-five had been allowed to opt for underground work in mining as an alternative to military service and then as from 29 July 1943 the age of twenty-five was changed to men of any age, with previous mining experience, and up to forty-five if none.

At the military registration on 18 September 1943, the registrants born in the last three months of 1925 were asked if they wished to be considered for placing in coalmining instead of the Forces. By 25 September, 13,078 men had opted or volunteered for mining. Of these, however, 4,156 withdrew or were unsuitable, and 3,530 had been placed in coalmining and other mining. In October the Ministry of Fuel and Power announced that men with previous underground mining experience who were now serving in the army at home were to be released for return to the coalmines. It was estimated that there would be 5,000 of them. However, 30,000 additional men would be needed in the industry before April 1944 and a further 20,000 later that year, and it was apparent that optants, volunteers and army releases would fall considerably short of this number.

So it was proposed that the only method of being able to deal with the problem was to direct 50,000 compulsorily to the coalmines during the course of 1944. These men would be drawn from amongst those born in or after 1918 where possible as most from this group were already in the forces, with the bulk of the men being taken from the first quarter of 1926 who would be due to register in December 1943. The first of these ballots was held on 14 December and twenty per cent were selected as a result.

It was later thought that the Bevin Boy scheme was an interesting social experiment, but its inception was bound to cause adverse reaction in many recruits and established miners. The question of a medical examination for young miners by a psychologist to decide whether they were temperamentally suited for coalmining before being balloted was put to the Minister, only to receive a straight answer of 'No'.

The unpopularity of the scheme led to a number of strikes by engineering apprentices in Tyneside, Clydeside and Yorkshire in March 1944. In June a debate in the House of Commons further rejected appeals of young men having joined pre-service organisations such as the Army and Navy Cadet Forces, as well as the Air Training Corps, that they should be exempt from the ballot. Ballots continued to be held at intervals until the end of the European War when the scheme was discontinued. A total of 21,800 Bevin Boys were recruited by this method.

Facts and figures taken from PRO: LAB 37/16 LAB 102/399.

Statement by Minister of Labour
and National Service in
the House of Commons on
Thursday, 2 December, 1943.

Compulsory recruitment of men for coalmining

My Right Hon. Friend the Minister of Fuel and Power announced in the House on 12th October that it would be necessary to call up men for the coalmines in the same way as they are called up for the Armed Forces. A scheme for the selection of men for this purpose has now been worked out and will begin to operate shortly. The selection will be made from men born on or after 1st January, 1918, who would otherwise be called up for the Armed Forces and are placed in medical grade I or grade II if their disability is foot defects only. My object has been to devise a scheme that will be recognised as fair and which would not place the duty upon the officials of my Department of selecting according to merit or suitability. I therefore propose to resort to the most impartial method of all, that of the ballot. A draw will be made from time to time of one or more of the figures from 0 to 9 and those men whose National Service Registration Certificate numbers happen to end with the figure or figures thus drawn by ballot will be transferred to coalmining. In the interests of fairness as between individuals the exclusion from the ballot will be limited to three classes of men only who I think it will be obvious must be kept for the other duties; they are (1) men accepted for flying duties in the R.A.F. or Fleet Air Arm: (2) men accepted as artificers in submarines; and (3) men in a short list of highly skilled occupations who are called up only for certain service trades and are not even accepted as volunteers for coalmining.

I propose to make arrangements for special medical examination of any man who claims that there are medical reasons why he is not fit for coalmining before he is sent to a Training Centre. Arrangements will be also be made for men to be medically examined again at a later stage with special reference to their fitness for underground work, and so far as possible this will be done at the Training Centre before they are finally posted to a colliery. Individuals whose call up to the Forces would be postponed on the grounds of exceptional hardship will not be transferred to coalmining.

Men selected for coalmining work who have had no previous experience of the industry will be given four weeks preliminary training both in classes and in actual underground practice at special Training Centres organised for the purpose by my Department in consultation with the Ministry of Fuel and Power. On completion of the training at the Training Centre they will be directed to working collieries for employment where (subject to special conditions in South Wales) they will be given further training for a fortnight before being employed on work below ground and for a period of at least four weeks after starting regular underground work they will come under the personal supervision of an experienced miner. There will be similar supervision for a sufficient time whenever they change from one class of work to another. Except in South Wales they will not go to work at the coal face until they have had at least four months underground experience. During the period of surface training they will be paid not less than the surface worker's rate. The men selected will be given an opportunity of stating a preference for a particular coal field, and an endeavour will be made to post men in accordance with their expressed preference, but it is impossible to guarantee this as a number of considerations must be kept in mind in posting men, such as the kind of coal produced, the productivity of the pit, and the availability of living accommodation. The Ministry of Fuel and Power will decide to what pits the men are to be directed.

In conclusion I want to say that the Government would not have resorted to this scheme of compulsion had it not been for the most urgent national necessity. There is no form of service which at this stage of the war is in greater need of young active recruits. Those who are chosen for transfer to coalmining will be doing their war service in a form that is as important as any, and I am sure that they will do their best to make a success of it.

Press Office,
Ministry of Labour and National Service,
8, St. James's Square, S.W.I.
2nd December, 1943

PRO:LAB 8/734

Letter from the Air Ministry (dated 20 October 1943) to the Ministry of Labour and National Service.

Air Ministry
Adastral House
Kingsway, W.C.2.
20th October, 1943

My dear de Villiers,

I have your letter of the 13th October, in which you discuss the question of implementing the Government decision to call up men for the coal mines as they are now called up for the Forces.

We are anxious, of course, to assist you as much as possible in your difficult task of creating the procedure of selection, and we certainly welcome your proposal to exclude from the ballot the men who have been accepted for flying service. This is undoubtedly sound, in view of the quality required in men for air crew duties With regard to the exclusion of the unasterisked tradesmen of certain categories, I assume you refer to the occupations, about 60 in number, which we refer to your Department where men apply for other air crew service. I gather that you propose to exclude them on the grounds that their technical and professional qualifications would be wasted if called up for coal mining.

Although we recognise the need for fair and impartial selection, we feel that the principle of the correct utilisation of man power is likely to be seriously impaired by your proposal to exclude no other types. We recall the criticism of the Beveridge Committee on mis-employment, and we have hitherto endeavoured to work to the rules laid down. If this general principle of making use of a man's skill and qualifications in the most suitable employment is now abandoned for coal mining recruitment, it seems to me it will be difficult to defend it in regard to ordinary enlistment to the Services. I do not think we should abandon at this stage the important principle that a man must be used in the most suitable employment, having regard to his education and training.

As you propose to select from the Allocation Register, it appears that State Bursars and Engineering Cadets will be excluded from the ballot. This being so, I am afraid we must register a strong protest against members of the Air Training Corps being included, having regard to their training in air subjects and trades. To include them and to post a proportion of them for coal mining would be a complete waste of this specialised training. I am sorry that I must press for men with Air Training Corps service to be excluded on the grounds that they have received this training specifically to prepare them for Royal Air Force and Fleet Air Arm Service.

I appreciate the points you make on the steps to be taken to prevent a man evading the ballot by volunteering for the forces after registration and subject to the men with A.T.C. service being excluded, we agree that after registration a man will not be accepted for ground service as a volunteer unless he is clear of the ballot. We take it that the rule that we do not take non A.T.C. volunteers from the younger age groups - 1923 onwards - should still apply.

With regard to the pre-registration volunteer, we would certainly wish to prevent the enlistment of a man who volunteers for the Services in order to evade being included later in the ballot, but equally we would not wish to be precluded from taking as volunteers A.T.C. cadets (having six months' enrolled service) or men, though non A.T.C., required for special ground categories, such as Aircraft Apprentices and recruits for Wireless trades, who hold the Postmaster General's certificate in radio telegraphy. There may be other small categories but if you would be prepared to consider sympathetically any application for relief from the normal rule which we may find it necessary to put to you, I think we can agree

Evening News, 7 January 1944
(reproduced by permission of the British Newspaper Library)

generally not to accept as volunteers, outside the categories I have mentioned, non A.T.C men in the pre-registration stage. By this means a sufficient curtailment of excessive volunteering would be achieved.

Nothing, of course, would prevent a man volunteering and being accepted for flying duties, either before or after registration.

Yours ever,

E. H. O'Donnell

PRO:LAB 6/226

Forms

EDL 94	Ministry of Labour & National Service Conditions of Employment and Training.
ED 383A	Ministry of Labour & National Service Direction Order and Schedule.
ED 383 (CTC)	Ministry of Labour & National Service Direction Order and Schedule
NS 6	Ministry of Labour & National Service Medical Summons.
ED 698	Ministry of Labour & National Service Coalmining Call-up.
ED 698 (Revised)	Ministry of Labour & National Service Coalmining Call-up.
ED 753	Notification of Release Group Number.
IO No. 1	Ministry of Fuel & Power Notification to appear before an Investigation Panel.
IO No. 3	Ministry of Fuel & Power Undertaking to agree to an interview before an Investigation Panel and to pay any fines imposed.
NS 2	Certificate of Registration.

MINISTRY OF LABOUR AND NATIONAL SERVICE
Training for employment in Coalmining

CONDITIONS OF TRAINING AT MINISTRY OF LABOUR AND NATIONAL SERVICE COALMINING TRAINING CENTRES WAGES AND ALLOWANCES

1. Weekly Rates. Trainees will be paid wages at the following rates:-

s.	d.		s.	d.	
45	0	p.w. at 17 years of age	65	0	p.w. at 19 years of age
47	6	17½	70	0	20
60	0	18	90	0	21

2. Deductions for unauthorised absence, including absence on Saturday, will be made at one-sixth of the weekly wage for each day of absence. Deductions for unauthorised absences for half a day will be one half of the appropriate daily rate.

3. **Travelling Expenses.**

(1) Fares will be paid from their homes to the centre area for men who have to leave home for training.

(2) Men who are able to live at home whilst in training, or have to be lodged at some distance from the Training Centre, will be paid any excess by which their daily travelling expenses exceed 6d. a day.

4. **Lodging Allowances and Settling-in Grants.**

(1) Men who have to leave home for training and who continue to maintain a household in their home area will be eligible for the normal transferred war-workers' living-away-from-home allowance of 3s. 6d. per night.

(2) Those who leave home for training but do not qualify for the allowance in (1) above will be paid a single settling-in grant of 24s. 6d.

STATUS OF TRAINEES

5. Trainees will be regarded as employed by and under contract of service to the Ministry of Labour and National Service and are insurable under the National Health and Unemployment Insurance Acts.

RULES IN FORCE AT MINISTRY OF LABOUR COALMINING TRAINING CENTRES

6. **Discipline**. For the proper efficiency of the Training Establishments, discipline must be maintained and the rules as set out herein complied with.

7. **Attendance**. Attendance must be punctual and regular, and work properly and diligently performed.

8. **Method of Payment.** Trainees should attend at the appointed pay station for weekly payments, but if they are unable to attend on account of sickness or other unavoidable absence, application should be made to the Training Establishment, in writing for payment either to a deputy, or through the nearest Local Office of the Ministry, or by post. Payment by

post should be requested only if the trainee is neither able to send a deputy nor to call at the nearest Local Office.

9. **Behaviour**. Gambling, betting, lending or borrowing money, drunkenness or any unseemly or disorderly conduct is forbidden.

10. **Tools, etc.** Tools, stores, equipment, clothing, and material for training exercises are provided for the purposes of training. These must not be taken away from the Establishment or left lying about and trainees may be held liable for lost tools.

11. **Property**. Government or other property must not be destroyed or damaged.

12. **Directions**. All directions from time to time issued by or on behalf of the Manager must be complied with.

13. **Baths**. Where Pithead baths are available trainees will be required to make payment by deduction from wages at the rate applicable to workers at the colliery to which the baths are attached. Trainees are required to provide their own towels and soap. (Workers in the mining industry are eligible for a supplementary soap ration.)

4. **Clothing**. Trainees should provide themselves with old but serviceable clothing to wear during training. This should include two pairs of thick woollen socks, two shirts (if possible, flannel), an old suit, two towels and an old mackintosh. Each trainee will be provided, free of charge, with a safety helmet and safety boots which he will be permitted to retain on the satisfactory completion of training. The surrender of 6 clothing coupons will be required in respect of the safety boots and these will be deducted from the 30 additional clothing coupons for which a trainee becomes eligible to provide himself with suitable working clothes on being directed to a colliery for further underground training. Protective overalls will be loaned to trainees for use during training.

15. **Trainees living away from home**. Trainees living away from home must take with them their ration books (including clothing book), gas masks, Health and Unemployment Insurance Books, and Form 3 D.S. (Part II) relating to Income Tax, if in possession of the trainee.

SICKNESS PAYMENTS AND REGULATIONS

16. Subject to the production of medical evidence of sickness (see paras. 18 and 19) and application as in para. 8, sick pay at the following rates is payable in addition to any National Health Insurance benefit to which trainees may be entitled whether they are sick at home, in lodgings or in hospital.

(1) **Trainees living in lodgings away from their homes.** Trainees living in lodgings away from their homes will be paid at the rate of 3s. 4d. a day (£1 0s. 0d. a week) from and including the first day of sickness.

(2) **Locals**. For absences of six working days or less local trainees will be paid as follows:-

Days absence	Sick Pay		Days absence	Sick Pay	
	s.	d.		s.	d.
1	Nil		4	10	0
2	Nil		5	15	0
3	5	0	6	20	0

For absences of more than six working days sick pay will be paid at the rate of 3s. 4d. a day (£1 0s. 0d. a week)..

17. Sick pay will be paid for the first three weeks of any period of continued absence certified in accordances with paras. 18 and 19 unless one week's notice in writing, to terminate the payment of any such allowances on a date before the end of the period of three weeks, has been given to the trainee by the Manager of the Centre. Sick pay is not payable after training has been terminated.

18. A medical certificate should be provided on the first day of sick absence but if this is not possible a written declaration, on a form obtainable from the Centre Manager, will be accepted to cover absence up to two days.

19. A medical certificate must be produced after an absence of two working days and this certificate should include the doctor's opinion as to the probable further period of absence from training. A further medical certificate will be required after an absence of six working days.

20. A declaring-off note must be produced at the end of the period of sickness.

21. All trainees who fall sick whilst living in lodgings away from home and require hospital treatment may be admitted to hospitals included in the Ministry of Health Emergency Hospitals Scheme. Such trainees may be required by the hospital to make a contribution towards the cost of their treatment.

ACCIDENTS DURING TRAINING

22. The provisions of the Workmen's Compensation Acts will apply to trainees who are incapacitated as a result of an accident during training.

23. Any trainee who sustains an accident, however slight, in the course of training, should report it at once to his instructor, or the First Aid Attendant. Failure to make a full report may lead to non-payment of workmen's compensation in respect of any absence which may result from the accident.

EMERGENCY ALLOWANCES

24. In addition to the payments described in paras. 16, 22 and 23 certain other allowances may be granted, at the Department's discretion, to trainees who are sick or incapacitated whilst living in lodgings away from their homes. In order to determine the amount of such emergency allowances it will be necessary for the Centre to be notified of the amount, if any, of National Health Insurance benefit to which a trainee is eligible. Accordingly trainees who are eligible should make a claim for National Health Insurance benefit as soon as they fall sick.

INCAPACITY ARISING FROM INJURIES
SUSTAINED BY ENEMY ACTION

25. The provisions of the Personal Injuries (Civilians) Scheme will apply to trainees who are incapacitated as a result of enemy action.

SAFETY RULES FOR NEW ENTRANTS TO COAL MINES

26. The following safety rules should be carefully noted by all trainees:-

(1) Before going underground in a safety lamp mine search your clothes for matches or forbidden articles.

(2) When riding in the cage hold on to the handrail and do not interfere with the gates.

(3) Behave in an orderly manner and observe instructions given by the colliery officials.

(4) Take care of your lamp.

(5) Walk at a safe distance behind or in front of moving tubs and keep on the outside of curves.

(6) Do not pass across the shaft bottom or through a fence.

(7) Keep behind tubs when taking them down a gradient.

(8) Do not place your hands and elbows between tubs—Other tubs may bump in behind and break your wrist or arm.

(9) Avoid loose clothing or scarves with loose ends which may be gripped by moving machinery, ropes or chains.

(10) Do not ride on ponies, nor on tubs unless authorised and instructed to do so.

(11) Do not couple or uncouple tubs in motion.

(12) Leave doors and brattice sheets exactly as you found them before passing through.

(13) Make yourself familiar with the codes of haulage signals in use.

(14) Keep your place of work tidy and free from obstruction.

(15) Never oil or grease machinery whilst in action.

(16) Always use the safety devices provided.

(17) Report at once any damage to safety devices or machinery fencing.

(18) Do not interfere with electrical or other apparatus.

(19) Regulations are made for your safety — Observe them.

(20) Small injuries if neglected may turn septic — report all injuries and have them properly dressed.

(21) Keep yourself fit and alert.

EMPLOYMENT AFTER TRAINING

27   On completion of training at the Ministry of Labour Training Centre trainees will be directed to a colliery for further training and employment.

28.   Trainees will be paid wages at the rate appropriate to the district for the occupation in which they are engaged.

29.   The national minimum weekly rates of pay are as follows:

	Underground		Surface	
	s.	d.	s.	d.
At 17 years of age	54	0	45	0
17½	57	6	47	6
18	70	0	60	0
19	75	0	65	0
20	80	0	70	0
21	100	0	90	0

30.   Fares will be paid for the initial journey from the Training Establishment to the colliery.

31.   Lodging allowances or settling-in grants will be payable on the conditions set out in para. 4.

MINISTRY OF LABOUR AND NATIONAL SERVICE

Emergency Powers (Defence) Acts, 1939-1940

DIRECTION ISSUED UNDER REGULATION 58A OF THE DEFENCE (GENERAL) REGULATIONS, 1939

NOTE—Any person failing to comply with a direction under Regulation `` `` of the Defence (General) Regulations, 1939, is liable on summary convic-`` `` to imprisonment for a term not exceeding three months, or to a fine not exceeding £100 or to both such imprisonment and such fine. Any person failing to comply after such a conviction is liable on a further conviction to a fine not exceeding five pounds for every day on which the failure continues.

To Mr.Stuart J.Chislett   Employment Exchange,

    67, Hookfield,   34, Upper High St. Epsom.

    Epsom.   (Date) 3/6/44

In pursuance of Regulation 58A of the Defence (General) Regulations, 1939, I, the undersigned, a National Service Officer within the meaning of the said Regulations, do hereby direct you to perform the services specified by the Schedule hereto (see overleaf) being services which, in my opinion, you are capable of performing.

This direction continues in force until the expiration of one calendar month after the date upon which you start to perform the services specified in the schedule hereto, or until it is withdrawn by a National Service Officer.

I hereby withdraw all directions previously issued to you under Regulation 58A of the said Regulations and still in force.

J. Ord

National Service Officer.

E.D. 383 (C.T.C.)   [P.T.O.

15

SCHEDULE

Employment as a trainee on underground coalmining work with the Ministry

of Labour and National Service at Prince of Wales Colliery,

Pontefract, Yorkshire

beginning on Monday, 12.6.44.   194

particulars of which are as follows :—

The rate of remuneration and conditions of service will be

60/- per week. Conditions of service will be

those standard at Coalmining Training Centre
concerned.

Further particulars Report direct to Training Centre

at the Colliery.

M5624 50M 4/44 CN&CoLtd 749 (2129) 6

NATIONAL SERVICE ACTS.

MINISTRY OF LABOUR AND NATIONAL SERVICE

Local Office, HANLEY

Registration No. RYT 256 1   2 4 MAR 44   (Date)

Mr. A. G. Perkin
School House
Abbotts Bromley
Stafford

DEAR SIR,

I have to inform you that in accordance with the National Service Acts you are required to submit yourself to medical examination by a medical board at 1 ──── on FRI day 3 1 MAR 1944 194 , at the Medical Board Centre,

If you wear glasses, you should bring them with you to the Medical Board.

On reporting for medical examination you should present this form and your Certificate of Registration (N.S. 2 or N.S.62) to the clerk in charge of the waiting room.

*A Travelling Warrant for your return journey is enclosed. Before starting your journey you must exchange the warrant for a ticket at the booking office named on the warrant. You should take special care of the return half of the ticket as in the event of loss you will be required to obtain a fresh ticket at normal fare at your own expense.

*If you reside more than six miles from the Medical Board Centre and travel by omnibus or tram your fare will be paid at the Centre.

Any expenses or allowances which may become payable to you in accordance with the scale overleaf will be paid to you on application when you attend at the Medical Board Centre.

Immediately on receipt of this notice, you should inform your employer of the date and time at which you are required to attend for medical examination.

If you are called up you will receive a further notification giving you at least three days' notice. You should accordingly not voluntarily give up your employment because you are required to attend for medical examination.

Your attention is directed to the Notes printed on the back of this Notice.

Yours faithfully,

H. P. BOND

N.S.6

*Delete if not applicable.

Manager.   [P.T.O.

SCALE

SUBSISTENCE ALLOWANCES.

Distance from home to place attended.	Amount.
	s. d.
Less than 10 miles	— —
10 miles and over but less than 20 miles	1 0
20 „ „ „ „ 40	1 6
40 „ „ „ „ 60	3 0
60 miles and over	4 6

When an absence overnight is unavoidable an allowance of 5s. 0d. will be paid in addition to the above scale.

ALLOWANCES FOR LOSS OF EARNINGS.

The officer at the Medical Board will be authorised to pay compensation for actual loss of earnings up to a maximum of 5s. 0d. to any person who claims such allowance in respect of pecuniary loss unavoidably suffered by attendance at a Medical Board. Any claimant who subsequently finds that this allowance is insufficient and desires to claim further compensation (subject to an overall maximum of 17s. 6d. a day) will be required to submit proof of loss on a claim form which may be obtained from the officer at the Medical Board or the office which issued this notice. Arrangements should be made, wherever possible, to avoid the loss of a full day.

NOTES

APPLICATIONS FOR POSTPONEMENT CERTIFICATES.

If, on the ground that exceptional hardship will ensue, you desire to apply for a certificate postponing your calling-up for service, you should, after the completion of your medical examination, ask the Clerk in Charge for an application form, N.S.13. The completed form must be returned to this Office within two days of the medical examination.

REGISTRATION AS A CONSCIENTIOUS OBJECTOR.

You are reminded that an application for provisional registration as a Conscientious Objector cannot ordinarily be accepted if made more than two days after completion of the medical examination.

CHANGE OF ADDRESS.

If when you receive this notice you have removed to a district a considerable distance from your address as entered on this form, or if by the day fixed for the medical examination you will have removed to such a district, you should not attend for medical examination, but should write *at once* to this Office and await further instructions. Unless such a communication is received from you no claim will be considered in respect of expenses incurred in travelling from an address other than that shewn on this form.

APPLICATIONS FOR ALLOWANCES.

Your attention is directed to the enclosed Form N.S. 139 regarding applications for family and dependants allowances and war service grants. You must tell the clerk when you attend for medical examination if you wish to make a claim.

M33895 500M 6/43 C.N.&Co.Ltd. 749 (110)

MINISTRY OF LABOUR AND NATIONAL SERVICE

....Regional Office.

....

2 OCT 1944

...............................(Date).

Dear Sir,

COALMINING CALL-UP.

The Government has decided that the essential man power requirements of the coalmining industry should be met by making underground coalmining employment an alternative to service in the Armed Forces and by directing to such employment a number of men who would otherwise be available for call-up for service in the Armed Forces.

Method of Selection.—The method of selecting men for direction to this employment has been made public. It is by ballot and is strictly impartial. Your name is amongst those selected.

Training.—Men who have had no previous experience of the coal-mining industry are to be given four weeks preliminary training on both surface and underground work at special Training Centres organised by the Ministry of Labour and National Service for the purpose. Men will then be directed to working collieries for employ-ment and will there receive (subject to special conditions in South Wales) a further fortnight's training before being employed on work below ground. Accordingly I have to notify you that it is proposed to direct you to attend in the near future at a Training Centre for a course of training with a view to subsequent employment in coalmining.

Conditions.—The enclosed leaflet E.D.L.94 gives information about training for and employment in coalmining.

Appeals.—You may appeal against this notification if you consider that there are any special circumstances connected with coalmining which would make it an exceptional hardship for you to be employed on that work. I have to remind you, however, that at the time of your medical examination under the National Service Acts you had an opportunity to apply for postponement of liability to be called up under these Acts. If therefore, you appeal against this notification, your appeal should show in what way you consider that employment in coalmining would be an exceptional hardship to you having regard to the fact that either you made no applica-tion for postponement of call up or your application has been determined and postponement, if granted, has expired. If there has been any material change in your circumstances since you previously had an opportunity of applying for postponement, or renewal of postponement you should call particular attention to this fact in your appeal.

If you decide to appeal, you may obtain a form on which to appeal (L.A.B.3 (C.M.D.)) from any Local Office of the Ministry of Labour and National Service, or you may appeal by letter. You should post your completed appeal *within four days* to the address

E.D 608 (Revised).

19

shown at the head of this letter. There will be no opportunity to
appeal at a later date when you are issued with a direction to a
training centre or to a working colliery.

If you make an appeal it will be put before the Local Appeal
Board and the Board will make a recommendation which will be
taken into account.

Unless it is decided after appeal to a Local Appeal Board that you
should not be directed to coalmining employment you will be
required to attend at a Training Centre.

Allocation.—Men are mainly required for coalmining employment
in Durham, Lancashire, Midlands, Northumberland, Notts, and
Derby, Yorkshire, Scotland and Wales.

No guarantee can be given of employment in any of these areas,
but individual preferences will be taken into account as far as
possible.

If you have a preference for employment in any of the areas
indicated you should write (even if you make an appeal against
this notification) to the address shown at the head of this letter
stating your preference and stating the address of any relatives or
friends in a coalmining district with whom you could live. If no
statement of preference is received within a week of the date of this
letter, it will be assumed that you do not wish to express any
preference. It will not be possible to take account of preference
which may be expressed subsequently.

On completion of training at the Training Centre you will be
directed to a working colliery. Any preference for employment in
a particular area which you may have expressed in reply to this
notification will then be taken into account as far as possible, even
if you have been required to undertake your training in another
area.

Yours faithfully,

for Regional Controller.

Mr. *L A MARTIN*

(32843) Wt. 51179—8010 50m 2/44 D.L. G. 373

3

The Luck of the Draw

The shock and disappointment of having received notification of selection by ballot for service in underground coalmining must have been very evident at the time, certainly for those who had set their hearts on joining the various branches of the Forces, many of whom had already completed several years of pre-service training in a Cadet Force.

Matters were made worse by friends and work mates from the office or factory, already having been called up or about to enter the Service of their choice. However, at the young age of eighteen, and about to leave home for the first time, anything would seem an adventure. With medicals over, usually conducted at the local territorial army drill hall, and appeals against the decision having failed, all that remained was to await the receipt of final instructions.

Inevitably this would arrive in the all too familiar O.H.M.S. brown envelope, which would contain a railway travel exchange voucher or warrant for travel to the station nearest to the colliery training centre, together with instructions, rules, regulations and the official notice of direction which outlined the penalties of fines, imprisonment or even both for failing to comply with the order.

The day would finally arrive to set off on this new adventure. On the train journey one might have met up with others in a similar plight, but certainly when alighting from the train at the final destination it soon became apparent that with others standing about looking somewhat bewildered, one was not alone. In most cases a Ministry of Labour Official would be there to meet the new recruits, and to organise the final stage of the journey either to a miners' hostel or allocation to a private residence where no hostel was available.

The Miners' Hostels were purpose built and known as the 500 Type Hostel, to cope with the influx of Bevin Boys at Training Centres and major collieries, and were managed by the National Service Hostels Corporation Limited. Part of the complex built of brick was known as the Welfare Block and housed the administration staff, dining room, three lounges, games room, quiet reading room and sick quarters.

The sleeping accommodation would be in Nissan huts with interlinked walkways to the toilets and showers as well as to the welfare block. There would be up to fifty-two Nissan huts, each with twelve beds and lockers. The beds measured two feet six inches in width, with an allocation of four blankets, three sheets, three pillow slips and three terry towels per person. In addition the locker unit contained three coat hangers, a soap dish, beaker, ash tray and mat.

Upon arrival you would be expected to hand in your ration book in exchange for a weekly issue of a book of meals tickets. The standard weekly charge of twenty-five shillings would cover the cost of accommodation and fifteen main meals, two on weekdays and three on Sundays. It was, however, the Government's policy that the pit head canteens should be used as much as possible, but if the third meal was not taken at the pit, this could be taken at the hostel at the cost of one shilling. In addition a 'snack' or 'snap' for consumption in the pit would consist of meat sand-wiches or sausage rolls, bread and butter, and piece of cake, or bun, or biscuits and tea could be obtained at the tea bar for the same cost. Thus a man could pay up to thirty-three shillings and sixpence for three main meals and the take-away 'snack' or 'snap'. In addition to these charges there was another two shillings to pay out for the laundry. However, life in these hostels was no holiday camp and understand-ably was subject to discipline, but there were advantages or disadvantages over those who were billeted out into private homes. Hostels provided many additional benefits such as regular meals and snacks, hot showers, recreational facilities and medical treatment, which one would not acquire by being billeted in a private house, many of which were miners' small terraced houses which were invariably spotless, where on the other hand one could enjoy good home cooking and often be treated as one of the family. If there were not pit head baths available at the colliery, it would mean taking a hot bath in the tin bath in front of a roaring fire. The fire was usually kept going throughout the year for this purpose, coal being provided free to the household of married miners. The only other inconvenience would be to trek down to the end of the garden in order to use the toilet, no joke on a cold winter's night. Lodging Allowances were agreed by the Ministry of Labour with the local landladies, which after various deductions, left very little out of the pay packet for oneself.

The following day all newcomers would be issued with a safety helmet, over-alls, steel-capped boots, gym shoes, vests and a padlock and key, retaining only the safety helmet and boots at the end of the training period. The surrender of six clothing coupons was required in respect of the safety boots, which would be de-ducted from the entitlement of the thirty additional clothing coupons allowed to trainees in order to obtain suitable working clothes on being directed to a colliery. In addition a supplementary soap ration and extra bread rations were issued.

The four weeks' training, described in the chapter on training, quickly passed and the day arrived to move on to the allocated colliery, when once again accommodation would be either in a miners' hostel or private billets.

A further two weeks' training took place before being allocated a specific job, invariably under the wing of an experienced miner, as it would be some time before being let loose to work on one's own. A Bevin Boy had to prove himself, for a young lad, who had just come from a background and way of life totally alien to the coalmining industry, was bound to be treated with caution and suspicion, as very often life and limb would be at risk as a result of careless actions. Gradually the Bevin boy would come to be accepted and would be placed on any variety of jobs, although invariably this would be below ground where the labour was needed.

The pay and conditions were far from good to say the least, but on occasions where breakdowns and shortage of railway trucks occurred, there would be no loss of pay providing one reported for work.

Coalmining, being a strong unionised industry, naturally expected Bevin Boys to become members. This of course caused considerable friction in some areas by posing a threat on those who had no wish to join; some even walked out and absconded. Leave and holidays left much to be desired, whilst Christmas Day was a general holiday, one was expected to start work again immediately after. For many this meant travelling a considerable distance, and wartime travel such as it was, resulted in overstaying leave of absence, with disciplinary action taken against the many offenders. Being employed under the Emergency Powers Act meant appearing before the Regional Investigating Officer and Colliery Management with Trade Union representation, inevitably resulting in loss of pay and a fine. In some cases the unfortunate offender would be brought before the local Magistrates and fined at the rate of £2 for every day of absence with the threat of imprisonment for non-payment.

Facts taken from PRO: WORKS 22/186 LAB 8/734.

North-Eastern Region -
Prince of Wales Colliery, Pontefract.

Trainees travel by train depart St. Pancras 10.00 a.m. arrive Pontefract (Baghill Station) 4.37 p.m., change at Sheffield.

Men should assemble at top of No. 6 Platform at 9.15 a.m. and look out for Reception Officer with armlet.

Birmingham Post, 14 March 1944

Service in Mines

In Sheffield a young man has been sentenced to three months' imprisonment for refusing to obey a National Service direction to go down a coal mine. Last week a similar case of refusal came before the Birmingham Stipendiary, but was adjourned pending a medical examination, which may or may not show that there exists good grounds for setting the direction aside. In each case the objection to work in a pit was based by the defendant on the same reasons; there was no plea of conscientious objection to war work, but a preference for a different form of service. One must feel some sympathy with the Birmingham objector, who had set his heart on service in the Royal Marines. The Sheffield objector urges that he could be more useful as an electrician. But in each case an individual was demanding that his own wishes should override a direction of the Ministry of Labour. When the decision was taken to enrol the requisite number of recruits for the mines by ballot, it was easy to foresee that objections of this nature would arise with much to be said in favour of some of them. But it is clear that public policy demands their rejection. The choice by ballot was introduced because it was judged expedient in the peculiar circumstances of the coal-mining industry. Without some such method there would inevitably be very harmful suspicions of 'wire pulling' to gain the exemption of this or that young man with influential connections. Once it be decided that recruiting the ranks of miners is as important as recruiting the Fighting Forces at this stage of the war, the Government must have a free hand in finding the recruits; individual preferences can count for nothing. The young men who obstinately contend that they should be given the choice are demanding as a right what is merely a privilege and one that can be granted only when conditions are favourable. If the objector is so self centred that he can see only his personal point of view, as sharp a sentence as in the Sheffield case may be needed to widen his vision. National Service cannot always be so arranged as to suit individual tastes.

During the first year of the Bevin Boy scheme 500 young men were prosecuted for refusal to obey the Direction Order, of whom 147 were actually sent to prison.

Coal Mining Ballot

December 1943 to May 1945

14 December 1943	0 & 9
15 January 1944	6 & 9
29 January 1944	2 & 5
16 February 1944	7
1 March 1944	2
16 March 1944	64
31 March 1944	9
15 April 1944	8
8 May 1944	13
20 May 1944	8
3 June 1944	5
20 June 1944	1
10 July 1944	1
24 July 1944	9
5 August 1944	3
19 August 1944	3
2 September 1944	0
16 September 1944	4
7 October 1944	8 & 9
18 October 1944	1 & 2
1 November 1944	0 & 2
22 November 1944	4 & 6
6 December 1944	8
20 December 1944	6
3 January 1945	0
17 January 1945	30
5 February 1945	37
19 February 1945	74
5 March 1945	23
23 March 1945	40
6 April 1945	33
23 April 1945	11
7 May 1945	36 Cancelled

Ballot selection was taken from last digit or digits of Registration Number.

PRO:LAB 45/96

Coal Mining Ballot
22nd November, 1944

Name	Regn. No.
Alcock, Norman Henry H.	NWZ.54
Allington, Dennis	HCR.18066
Allsopp, Leonard Jas.	BMD.5004
Anslow, John	DCB.3986
Arkell, Ralph Edward	SWF.6274
Attwood, John Arthur	CPF.55214
Austin, Peter Derek K.	SSN.10664
Ayriss, Stanley	CPF.53154
Bailey, Peter	WFZ.18464
Baker, Thomas Henry	BXX.51364
Barlow, Phillip Joseph	HCR.10894
Barnacle, Herbert R.	CPF.51134
Bate, Douglas Eric	HBP.5364
Baynham, Tom Edgar	WXX.37394
Beasley, John	ANR.31376
Benion, James Harold	BJV.9956
Bennett, Ernest	BJV.11554
Bennett, Wm. Geoffrey	WJK.14376
Bennett, Wm. Raymond	BRK.6476
Bissoni, Harold Hugh	UTR.2974
Bluck, Harold Leslie	WHB.6666
Bone, Peter	MJB.25704

-15-

Woodward, Douglas Leonard	KFB.7844
Woodward, Thos. Henry	NWZ.8236
Worthington, Ernest J.	CPF.57656
Wyse, Arthur	WHB.6616
Yates, Albert	BRK.6504
Yemm, Albert Stephen	NWZ.13264

The first and last of a fifteen page list showing alphabetically, Bevin Boy ballotees for the Midland Region during November 1944, (Note the ballot numbers for that month* were taken from those registration numbers ending in 4 or 6.)
* During December 1943 to May 1945, thirty-three ballots were conducted on a twice-monthly basis.

R.O.9A
EG   COALMINING TRAINING
The undermentioned have been allocated to a coalmining training centre in
your region to report on 29th January, 1945.
BIRLEY
Ballotees

Name	Local Office
WEBSTER J.	Aston
SMITH R.L.	"
Simmons B.	"
Lane J.E.	"
Hyde C.J.	"
Booth G.A.	"
Roe L.A.	"
Hughes P.	Birmingham
Simpson F.W.	"
Hill R.	Cradley Heath
Priest S.N.	" "
Wells W.	Handsworth
Hunt F.	"
Harrison A.	"
Bradbury E	"
Shaw H.M. C.M.D. action	Cancelled" 26/1
Smith J.	Sparkhill
While T.S.	"
Scott J.S.	"
Hughes R.	"
petts H.	"
Lea H.T.E.	"
Sawyer F.L. "	
Perry L.H.	Sparkhill
POLEY J.T.	"
ROCHESTER W.J.	"
BURN G.	Smethwick
NEW F.S.	"
COLE P.	"
HERBERT J.V.	Selly Oak
POOLE G.M.	"
SMITH W.	"
LANCASTER H.	"
WOOD P.C.J.	"
WYSE A.	Wednesbury
BENNETT W.G.	"
GARDNER E.A.	Washwood Heath
HARRIS R.	Redditch"
DANKS P.H.	" "
WALKER D.	Washwood Heath

                          (Sgd) J.E.D.
                          for Regional Controller,
                          16th January 1945
The Regional Controller,
NORTH EASTERN R.O.
M.R. Section, 3 JAN 1945
For information.
(Sgd) J.E.D.
Regional Controller, 16th January 1945

North Eastern Regional Office Coal Mining Training allocation of Bevin Boys to
(BIRLEY EAST) Colliery Training Centre in January 1945. Local Employment
Exchange Offices are given. PRO : LAB 45/95.

M. R. Section, (for the attention of Mr. Astbury)
<u>HALFORD BUILDINGS</u>

<u>MEN WHO REPORTED FOR TRAINING TO TUNNEL PIT 13.3.44</u>

	Name	Local Office	Remarks
B	Arnold, C. H.	Nuneaton	
O	Ashman, J.	"	
O	Bates, C.	Tamworth	
B	Bates, R.	Rugby	
B	Pickley, P. G.	Nuneaton	
B	Bill, F.	Staniforth Street, B'ham.	
B	Blaby, T.	Soho Road, Handsworth	
B	Bonehill, W. G.	Staniforth Street, B'ham.	
B	Bray, W.	Coventry	
B	Butwell, R. A.	West Bromwich	
V	Cartwright, W.	Bilston	
B	College, H.	Small Heath, Birmingham	
O	Conway, G. W.	Soho Road, Birmingham	
B	Churchill, A. T.	Ross-on-Wye	
O	Davies, S. C.	Tamworth	
B	Davies, S.	Smethwick	
B	Dean, L. G.	Staniforth Street, B'ham.	
B	Fellows, R. E.	Aston, Birmingham	
B	Fouldling, J. E.	Aston, Birmingham	
B	Garbett, D.	Walsall	
B	Green, R.	Cradley Heath	
B	Griffiths, H.	W'wood Heath Road, B'ham.	
O	Gwilliam, C.	Walsall	
V	Hammonds, W.	Bilston	
B	Hancock, L.	Nuneaton	
B	Harwood, I. G.	Kenilworth	
O	Hibbs, J.	Cannock	
B	Hickman, R. L.	Tipton	
B	Hodnett, J.	Smethwick	
O	Humphreys, N.	Aston, Birmingham	
	Kirby, W. J.	Swadlincote	
O	Layton, J. E.	Hereford	
O	Lovekin, A.	Small Heath, B'ham.	
B	Manby, D. F.	Staniforth Street, B'ham.	
B	McNeill, C.	Aston, Birmingham	
O	North, G.	Brierley Hill	
V	Oakley, F.	"	
	O'Connor, P.	Leicester	
B	Peace, J. A.	Belly Oak, B'ham.	
B	Pearcy, R.	Small Heath, B'ham.	
B	Phillips, A.	Birmingham	
B	Potter, W.	"	
B	Powell, E.	Small Heath, Birmingham	
O	Proctor, W.	Bedworth	
B	Randall, R. A.	Staniforth Street, B'ham.	
B	Rollins, J. S.	West Bromwich	
B	Sallis, G. L.	Evesham	
B	Simmonds, N.	Small Heath, Birmingham	
V	Smith, R.	Hereford	
V	Strong, G.	Bilston	
O	Taylor, H. S.	Atherstone	
O	Taylor, L. J.	Tamworth	
O	Thompson, M.	Coventry	
B	Thornewell,	A. Selly Oak, Birmingham	
B	Turner, S.	Bedworth	
B	Walters, H.	Oldbury	
O	Wells, A.	Brierley Hill	
B	Woodyatt, S.	West Bromwich	
B	Woolley, R. E.	Coventry	
ex H.M.F.	Blake, W. G. T.	Battersea	

```
Ex H.M.F.   Bradshaw, H.      South'ton
ex H.M.F.   Howe, A.          Guildford
ex H.M.F.   Selby, K. S.      Kings Langley
ex H.M.F.   Tovey, J.         Yardley, Birmingham
B           Aston, N.         Dudley
O           Bytheway, J. H.   Dudley
V           Farrington, R.    Cannock
ex H.M.F.   Sharpe, L.        H.M.F.
ex H.M.F.   Flint, L. W.        "
B           Raybould, H. G.   Cradley Heath
B           Bellamy, H. J.    Staniforth Street, B'bam.
O           Bygrave, G.       Small Heath, Birmingham
O           Forde, J.         Stratford-on-Avon
O           Fullwood, J.      Wallsall
            Coulthard, R.     Leicester
B           Toon, F. J.       Stanifortb Street, B'ham.
B           Harvey, A.        Leamington
```

Birmingham Regional Office listing names of Bevin Boys who reported for training to Tunnel Pit (HAUNCHWOOD) Colliery Training Centre in March 1944 and local Employment Exchange Offices given. (The prefix markings of B, O or V are self evident.) PRO: LAB 45/95

COPY

                          AND NATIONAL SERVICE.

                                            Headquarters F.D.3
Regional
xxxxxxx   R.O.9A.   Prince of Wales Hotel.
                                                      SOUTHPORT.
                          COAL MINING TRAINING
The undermentioned have been allocated to the North Staffs E.T.E. to report on the
5th February, 1943.

Name	Date of Birth	Address	Local Office
Thirwall, D.	4.6.20	84, Wharf St.	Burslem
Lawton, F.	17.12.26	4, New Hayes Rd. Tunstall	"
Steed, A.B.	7.12.26	1, Park Terrace. "	"
Yates, A.	27.10.26	41, Birds Meadows, Pensnett.	Brierley Bill
Green, J.	12.10.17	158, Watling St.	Brownhills
Nutting, W.F.	6.7.26	129, Lichfield Rd.	"
Evans, B.S.	26.11.26	2, Pearl Cottages, Chorley	Bridgnorth
Johnson, L.B.	7.11.20	7, Batton St. Bradley.	Bilston
Jennings, W.	23.10.26	28, Watson Rd. Woodcross	"
Gripton, R.	6.9.24	1, Carlton Avenue	"
Carrington, A.E.	12.2.21		3, Bank St. Bradley. "
Bennett, E.	13.11.26	6, Oxford St.	"
Benion, J.B.	10.1.23	27, Mount Rd. Lanesfield	"
McGee, W.A.	25.4.26	14, Temple St. Bilston	"
Barvey, A.	1.6.22	13, Connaught Rd. 8t.Chads	"
Bigginson, J.B.	27.1.27	28, Borse Rd. Alton.	Cheadle
Cope, W.	28.11.22	Ipstone Park, Ipstones	"
Edwards, S.A.	25.7.21	Mobberley Cottages, Mobberley	"
Bates, C.J.	17.1.27	10, Watling St. Bridgtown	Cannock
Morgan, R.	3.1.27	165, Stafford Rd.	"
Willingale, C.F.	2.8.26		40, Beeches Rd. East. Cradley Heath
Tromans, A.V.	28.2.24	11, Firth Drive, Narrow Lane	"
Newell, A.D.	28.12.26	32, Stafford Rd.	Darlaston

Name	DOB	Address	Location
Baggott, J.	13.5.24	5, Biddlestone Place.	Darlaston
Stokes, W.D.	7.11.24	20, Watson Grn. Rd.	Dudley
Rowley, W.L.	6.3.19	51, Clarence St. Upper Gornal	"
Rutter, R.W.	3.12.21	22, French Rd.	"
Lawrence, K.J.	19.12.26	48, Bridgewater Crescent	"
Homer, R.W.	6.1.27	35, New Rd.	"
McCue, J.	31.12.26	225, Milton Rd. Sneyds Grn.	Hanley
Masefield, F.W.	7.6.20	10, Adam St. Milton	Hanley
Dunn, S.J.	12.1.21	112, Belmont Rd. Etruria	"
Rowley, H.	31.8.20	9, Commercial Rd.	"
Wood, G.	21.9.20	77, Alfred St.	"
Green, R.	22.10.24	17, Abbey Rd. Abbey Hulton.	"
Lowe, A.	26.12.26	28, Thomas St. Talke	Kidsgrove
Pownall, J.	12.7.26	135, Congleton Rd. Butt Lane.	"
Barlow, E.C.	5.1.27	Hayes Gate, Huline End Nr. Burton.	Leek
Nuttall, L.N.	20.10.20	3, Tupp Stepo, Newtown.	Market Drayton
Treherne,D.R.E.	28.1.26	17, Shrewsbry Rd. Edgmond	Newport (Salop)
Harrioon, J.G.	11.1.27	6, Church Lane, Knutton.	Newcastle (S)
Leese, H.	19.2.26	60, WilBon St.	"
Roberto, R.	13.11.26	11, Victoria St.	Wolstanton
Johnson, R.	17.12.26	7, Cleve Ave. Porthill	"
Punohon, D.B.	14.12.	26 Granville Etruria Rd. "	
Steele, D.J.	10.12.26	11, Hartshill Avenue.	Oakengates
Potts, R.	8.1.27	Brambleside Cottaqe.	Rugeley
Johnoon, N.T.	23.12.26	24, First Ave.	Stafford
Handley, G.	22.12.24	7, Green Lane.	"
Clift, F.G.	19.2.27	52, New Park St.	Shrewsbury
Bennett, E.C.	19.1.10	13, Clinton Craven Arms	"
Crookford, W.H.	25.9.20	33, Waterloo St.	Tipton
Fullord, D.H.	2.12.26	65, Furnace Parade.	"
Harvey, J.B.	20.11.26	67, Cotterells Rd.	"
Walker, A.	31.10.26	34, Horton St.	"
Wellings, E.	25.9.21	7, Laurel Rd. Summerhill	"
Yale, D.	14.4.22	57, Laburnum Rd.	"
Fox, J.T.	9.12.26	48, Young St.	West Bromwich
Purcell, S.	13.1.26	Gantons Bank	Whitchurch
Kenrick,H.(Jnr)	10.3.25	41, Ladbarge Lane.	Wednesbury
Gough, D.	11.6.26	59, Booth St.	Walsall
Hammond, A.	5.7.23	48, Walsingham St.	"
Shaw, J.	30.12.26	53, Viqo Rd.	"
Russell, T.J.	20.10.26	68, Staghill, Harden	"
Baynham, T.E.	23.10.26	4, Myatt Close	Wolverhampton
Joyce, T.	24.4.26	9, St. Mary's Terrace	"
Hill, J.H.	4.5.20	50, Alma St.	"
Gwinnett, I.D.	11.4.26	159, Lea Rd.	"
Wilmot, S.F.	15.2.26	65, Dartmouth St.	"
Jameo, L.W.	18.11.25	Bk.64, ChurchSt.	Bilston
Pugh, J.G.	7.11.26	17, Broad St.	Wolverhampton
Richards, W.A.	3.5.21	132, Wood End Rd.	"
Harriss, B.W.	24.8.20	10, Vicaraqe Terrace.	Walsall
Lakin, B.	19.1.27	Wellhouse Farm, Now Cop.	Biddulph

Regional Control,
25th January, 1945.

Regional Headquarters Coal Mining Training allocation of Bevin Boys to North Staffs E.T.E. (KEMBALL) Colliery Training Centre in February 1945. Dates of birth, addresses and local Employment Exchange Offices are given.
PRO : LAB 45/95

4

Miners' Hostels

The National Service Hostels Corporation Limited, managed on behalf of the Ministry of Fuel and Power, hostels were primarily built for the accommodation of ballotees. The construction took place in three stages according to the urgency of the requirements in different areas, but by the time Stage III had been reached, the ballots had been suspended and fourteen hostels were either given up or not brought into use. Many hostels were completed months before the Ministry of Fuel and Power were in a position to draft miners, with the result of many lying empty.

The position of the availability of hostels in July 1945 is shown on the Ministry of Works chart. Redundant hostels given up by the Ministry of Fuel and Power were mainly used for Dutch and Polish refugees.

The second chart produced by the Ministry of Labour shows the state of miners' hostels in December 1945.

However, the break down of the coalmining regions vary considerably between the two charts.

July 1945	December 1945
Alloa	Sauchie
Barnsley I	Broadway
Bentley I	Queens Drive
Castleford I	Hightown
Chester le Street	Pelaw Bank
Doncaster I	Sandringham
Maltby	Bramley
Mansfield East	Abbott Road
Newcastle-under-Lyme	Knutton
Sedgefield	Ferryhill
South Moor	New Kyo (new centre)
Stoke on Trent I	Smallthorne
Tamworth	Watling Street

Hostel	Capacity	Number of Residents (July 1945)	Remarks
ENGLAND			
Alfreton	200	155	
Askem	350	-	Evacuees 7/44 to 2/45
Miners to 6/45 (Dutch)			
Ashington	300	168	
Barnsley I	400	344	
Barnsley II	250	-	Evacuees 7/44 to 5/45
(Dutch)			
Bentley I	500	306	
Bentley II	250	-	Dutch
Cannock I	500	414	
Cannock II	350	-	Miners till 7/45
Castleford I	500	283	
Castleford II	300	-	Evacuees 1/45 to 5/45
(Dutch)			
Chester le Street I	250	159	
Chester le Street II	250	90	
Coalville	200	-	Transferred to M.A.F. 2/45
Coventry II	500	157	Miners from Keresley 1/45
Creswell	500	-	Miners 8/44 to 6/45
Crook	250	81	
Doncaster I	500	415	
Doncaster II	200	-	Evacuees 7/44 to 5/45
(Dutch)			
Easington	600	255	
Eastwood	300	280	
Haydock	250	176	
Hucknall	150	135	
Keresley	500	-	Miners 5/44 to 1/45 Evacuees from St. Helens 2/45 to 6/45
Leadgate	350	106	
Maltby	450	232	Evacuees 7/44 to 3/45
Mansfield East	500	170	Evacuees 7/44 to 2/45
Mansfield North	500	354	
Mexborough I	500	319	
Newcastle-under-Lyme	500	315	
Rotherham	200	-	

Hostel	Capacity	Number of Residents (July 1945)	Remarks
St. Helens	250	168	Evacuees 7/44 to 2/45
Sedgefield	500	261	
South Moor	600	341	
Stoke I	500	324	
Sutton-in-Ashfield	200	-	Not wanted by miners
Tamworth	200	179	
Wakefield	200	-	Dutch
Walkden	350	160	
Walsall	500	-	Polish Nautical School
Whitburn	150	-	
Woodhouse	250	159	
Worksop I	500	164	
WALES			
Aberdare	250	156	
Bryncethin	200	105	
Oakdale	500	127	
Pontypridd	300	182	
Ystradmynach	350	200	
SCOTLAND			
Alloa	100	51	
Armadale	250	145	
Comrie	200	140	
Cowdenbeath	450	352	
Dalmellington	150	60	
Falkirk	250	95	
Kirkconnel	250	90	
Methilhill	200	167	
Muiredge	200	185	
Newtongrange	250	221	
Stirling	400	316	
Townhill	500	174	
Wilsontown	100	-	Not wanted by miners

Hostel	Date Opened	Capacity	Number of Residents (Dec 1945)
SCOTTISH REGION			
Armadale	3 Jun 1944	250	107
Ashington	11 Dec 1944	320	88
Comrie	21 Feb 1944	200	102
Cowdenbeath	30 Nov 1944	450	182
Crook	21 May 1945	250	64
Dalmellington	2 Oct 1944	150	47
Easington	26 Jun 1944	610	136
Falkirk*	13 May 1944	240	114
Ferryhill	20 May 1944	500	217
Leadgate	11 Dec 1944	250	54
Methilhil	28 Feb 1944	200	91
Muiredge	6 Mar 1944	200	125
New Kyo	22 Jul 1944	600	217
Newtongrange	13 May 1944	250	183
Pelaw Bank	27 May 1944	250	177
Ryton	9 Apr 1945	200	65
Sauchie	11 Sep 1944	100	51
Stirling	10 Jun 1944	400	124
Townhill	13 May 1944	500	93
Scottish Region 19		*5,920*	*2,237*

*Includes an unknown number of industrial workers. This Hostel was transferred to Industrial (Ministry of Labour) on 1 Jan 1946.

Hostel	Date Opened	Capacity	Number of Residents (Dec 1945)
NORTH WEST REGION			
Haydock	25 May 1944	250	140
St. Helens	5 Feb 1945	250	76
Walkden	2 Oct 1944	360	86
North Western Region 3		*860*	*302*
MIDLAND REGION			
Cannock 1	27 May 1944	500	294
Knutton	18 Sept 1944	500	186

Hostel	Date Opened	Capacity	Number of Residents (Dec 1945)
Nuneaton	28 Jan 1945	500	98
Smallthorne	27 May 1944	500	250
Watling	20 May 1944	200	144
Midland Region 5		*2200*	*972*

NORTH EASTERN REGION

Abbot Road, Mansfield	27 May 1944	500	341
Alfreton	4 Dec 1944	200	100
Bramley *	5 Jun 1944	450	142
Broadway	21 Jul 1944	400	208
Eastwood	11 Aug 1944	320	226
Hightown	13 May 1944	500	140
Hucknall	11 Aug 1944	150	134
Mexborough	20 May 1944	500	232
Queens Drive	27 May 1944	500	226
Sandringham	6 May 1944	500	296
Woodhouse	20 May 1944	250	106
Worksop	17 Jul 1944	400	114
North Eastern Region 12		*4670*	*2265*

*Miners transferred to Worksop on 17 July 1944. Bramley was re-opened for Miners on 18 March 1945.

SOUTH WESTERN REGION

Aberdare	19 Feb 1945	250	108
Bryncethin*	8 Jan 1945	200	67
Oakdale	6 May 1944	500	95
Pontypridd	6 Nov 1944	310	110
Ystrad Mynach	22 Jul 1944	360	127
South Western Region 5		*1620*	*507*

*Closed 19 January 1946.

SUMMARY

Region	No.	Total Capacity	Number of Residents (Dec 1945)
Scottish Region	19	5920	2237
North Western Region	3	860	302
Midland Region	5	2200	972
North Eastern Region	12	4670	2265
South Western Region	5	1620	507
Total Opened	44	15270	6283

The Regions shown for Miners Hostels differ from those of the Coalmine Regions.

The total figures quoted for the number of residents (Dec 1945) are those of coalmining employees only, whereas the majority of Miners Hostels also accommodated a proportion of industrial workers or service personnel which is not included.

Hostels Closed

Hostel	Capacity	Opened	Closed
Askern	360	19 Feb 1945	2 Jun 1945
Bridgetown	350	14 May 1945	15 Jul 1945
Chester-le-Street	250	29 Jan 1945	1 Sept 1945
Creswell*	500	12 Aug 1944	2 Jun 1945
Forest Town	500	27 May 1944	17 Jul 1944
		Miners transferred to Mansfield (Abbot Road). Re-opened 13 Mar 1945	17 Aug 1945
Kirkconnel	250	25 Sept 1944	22 Dec 1945
Mobile	80	1 Nov 1943	1 Oct 1944
Warmsworth	200	13 Mar 1945	31 May 1945

*Hostel transferred to the Ministry of Labour.

The hostels built at Keresley, Coventry and Carlton Road, Barnsley, withdrew from the programme and were taken over by the Ministry of Health.

Facts and figures taken from PRO: WORKS 22/186, WORKS 22/188, LAB 22/63

Miners' Hostels

Notes for New Residents

You have just arrived at this Hostel and may find things a little strange at first, particularly if you have not lived away from home before. You will find that you will soon settle down, make friends and feel at home.

The members of the Hostel staff, from the Manager downwards, will do their best to make you comfortable and happy and, if you have any trouble or difficulty at any time, do not hesitate to go to them. The names of the senior officers of the Hostel are shown on the Notice Board.

In running the Hostels we do not have a great number of rules and regulations. We prefer to rely on the good sense of the residents. There are some rules, of course, but the idea behind them is to promote the comfort and well-being of the residents as a whole and it is in the interest of all the residents to conform to them. In a few days you will become familiar with the running arrangements of the Hostel, but a glance through the following notes will give you a general picture.

Meal Service

When you arrive here you hand in your Ration Book. You are given a membership card and a book of Meal Tickets to last until the end of the week. This book entitles you to lodgings and two main meals every day with an additional meal on Sundays. You hand over a ticket when you receive a meal and you pay for the book weekly. If you are away, on prior notice, from the Hostel for a complete day (24 hours) or several complete days, the charges for the week are reduced.

If you happen to be away from your work for any good reason, you can obtain an additional meal by purchasing a ticket on showing your membership card. Snacks at low charges are issued from the Canteen for those who wish to take them to work. A Tea Bar, serving light refreshments at reasonable charges, is open at certain hours each day.

The times when the meals are served are fixed to suit your working hours. It is a great help to the catering staff if you attend promptly for meals at the times shown and also if you take your dirty crockery to the clearing tables. At some of our Hostels the losses and breakages of cutlery and crockery are very heavy. Apart from regretting such waste in war time, we have great difficulty in getting replenishments; so, please help as much as you can in this matter.

Guests

If, at any time, you want a male friend or relative to spend a few days at the Hostel, the Manager will arrange to put him up at a reasonable charge provided accommodation is available. Give the Manager as much notice as possible of the proposed visit and remember, it can only be arranged if beds are available.

There is no objection to your having an occasional guest in the Hostel for a meal or entertainment, but consult the Manager first. Don't overdo this or it might cause inconvenience to your fellow residents.

Sick Bay and Health Insurance

The Hostel has a Sick Bay, with a Nurse in attendance, for those suffering from slight ailments.

You no doubt have a Medical Card and you would be well advised to change over to a local doctor. It is better to do this straight away rather than wait until you are ill. This will not stop you getting free treatment from your own doctor if you are sent home. A list of doctors and the address of the local Insurance Committee are posted on the Notice Board. You have a free choice.

A transferred war worker is entitled to a sickness maintenance allowance from the Ministry of Labour and National Service if he stays at the Hostel during a short illness during which he does not receive wages. A letter from the Welfare Officer will put this right for you. If you are too ill to collect the benefit yourself, a 'deputy' form can be obtained and the money brought to you.

In cases of need, the Ministry gives other forms of assistance, e.g. a free warrant for a sick worker to return home or for a near relative to visit him. A pocket-money allowance may also be paid to a transferred worker who goes into hospital. You can get full information about these allowances by inquiry at the nearest Employment Exchange.

New Friends

The Hostel should not be a self-centred independent unit but an addition to an old established community. Your work will bring you into contact with fresh people in new surroundings. These new associates will be glad to welcome you into the social life of their community. In particular, you will find a warm welcome awaiting you at the Miners' Institute.

Laundry

Arrangements are made for you to get your laundry done at reasonable prices. Full particulars about this are shown on the Notice Board.

Official Address

When you write to your friends and relatives, ask them to address all your letters and parcels to the official address which is shown on the Notice Board. A list of Registered letters and parcels for residents is put on the Notice Board. Ordinary letters are put in racks and, when passing, you can ask at the office whether there are any letters for you.

Residents' Committee

The residents should form a Committee at each Hostel, which concerns itself firstly with the general interests of the residents and secondly with sports and entertainments. The Committee looks after your interests and helps the Hostel in many ways. It will help the Committee to do good work if you will take an interest in it.

The following paragraph was printed on the back page of the booklet.

In the Royal Navy they talk about a ship being a happy ship. You may remember it in the film 'In Which We Serve'. We want this Hostel to be a happy Hostel. We know that much depends on the staff and how they run the place, but a lot depends also on you.

National Service Hostels Corporation Limited.

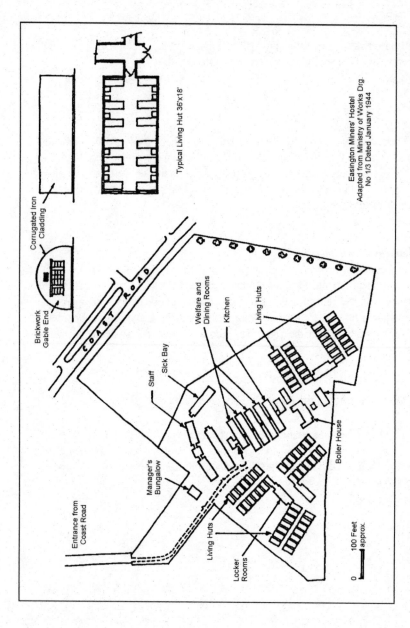

Corrugated Iron Cladding

Brickwork Gable End

Typical Living Hut 36'x18'

COAST ROAD

Entrance from Coast Road

Manager's Bungalow

Staff

Sick Bay

Welfare and Dining Rooms

Kitchen

Living Huts

Boiler House

Living Huts

Locker Rooms

0   100 Feet
approx.

Easington Miners' Hostel
Adapted from Ministry of Works Drg.
No 1/3 Dated January 1944

The layout of Easington Miners' Hostel is typical of most constructed by the Ministry of Works throughout the United Kingdom.

WITHOUT PAYMENT AT THE TIME OF BOOKING.

NON-RECOVERABLE.

Form No. A/cs. 44D.

CHARGES PAYABLE BY:—
**MINISTRY OF LABOUR
& NATIONAL SERVICE**
Finance Department.
HESKETH PARK HYDRO,
SOUTHPORT, LANCS.

ISSUING OFFICE STAMP

HANLEY

EMPLOYMENT EXCHANGE

F 705464

**GOVERNMENT
TRAVELLING
WARRANT.**

Names of Passengers.... *PERKIN. H. G.*

Service/Authority† (See M.L.C. 22/90) ...... *T.A.*

Date............ *16/10/1944.* (Available only on this date.)

To the................ *L.M.S.* ......Railway Company
Please issue, without charge to the Bearer, ticket(s) as shown below :—

FROM........... *STOKE ON TRENT*

TO........... *RUGELEY*

for SINGLE / RETURN§ journey at *three-fourths* *Fares
(in words)............ *One* ......Tickets **3rd Class.**
(Children under 14 years to be entered as "Half" and no entry
to be made for children under 3 years of age.)

Signature of issuing Officer *J. Barlestones*

Departmental or other Rank *E.O.*

TO BE COMPLETED BY THE COMPANY.
...........................Tickets Nos......................3rd Class
issued over Route via...................................
at.....................................*Fares

Amount Payable	£	s.	d.

Date..........................Issued by.......................

§ Strike out word inapplicable.
* For rail journeys insert "three-fourths," "household removal" or "monthly
return" if available. For rail journeys exclusively on L.P.T.B. insert "ordinary."

This warrant is not
transferable. It must be
presented at the Booking
Office at the place of
departure, when a Ticket
or Tickets will be issued
in exchange.

Tickets must in every
case be issued via the
recognised direct and
cheapest route.

Any alteration in
this Warrant must be
initialled by a responsible
officer.

†**IMPORTANT:—**

EXACT PARTICULARS OF
SERVICE, AS SPECIFIED
IN THE RELEVANT
CODE AND CIRCULAR
INSTRUCTIONS, SHOULD
BE RECORDED HEREON.

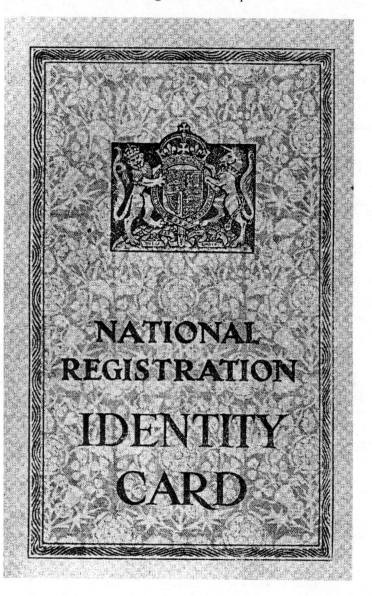

National Registration Identity Card issued to all United Kingdom citizens during the Second World War. This was stamped by the Ministry of Labour & National Service when Bevin Boys were employed in the coal mining industry.

MINISTRY OF FOOD

RATION BOOK
SUPPLEMENT

This is a Spare Book

YOU WILL BE TOLD
HOW AND WHEN TO USE IT

HOLDER'S NAME AND REGISTERED ADDRESS

Surname........ *HERRING*

Other Names..... *William R*

Address ..... *1 Walton Way*
Mitcham

If found, please return to

MITCHAM

FOOD OFFICE
7 JUL 1941

Date of Issue..............

L.61

NATIONAL REGISTRATION NO.

CNCZ | 37 | 1

Class and Serial No. of Ration Book already held

RB1 PP 609997

R.B. 9

Ration Book Supplement issued by the Ministry of Food to all those employed in heavy industry, an additional Cheese Ration. Bevin Boys were no exception.

SUPPLEMENTARY CLOTHING COUPON SHEET SC5G

UH 990893

Name HENRY GEORGE PERKIN
(BLOCK LETTERS)

Address School House Abbots Bromley
(BLOCK LETTERS)

(town) .... (county) STAFFS.

Nat. Reg'n (Identity Card) No. OTXI / 41 / 6

IMPORTANT.—These coupons may not be used unless the holder's name, full postal address, and National Registration (Identity Card) Number have been plainly written above IN INK.

Supplementary Clothing Coupons were issued to Bevin Boys to allow the purchase of industrial clothing and boots.

5

Training

Training Centres were subsequently opened with the first five on 28 December 1943, followed by three more in January 1944, with a further three in February. The initial training period of four weeks' duration, known as stage 'A', was set up by the Ministry of Labour, and would be given to ballotees, optants and volunteers.

The curriculum would consist of a 44-hour week, divided into the following activities: physical training 25 per cent, class work and mine visits 25 per cent, surface training 20 per cent and underground training 30 per cent. The object of this initial training was an introduction to underground conditions of employment, pit sense, safety measures and a sense of comradeship. Physical training was essential in order to develop muscles for the type of manual work involved.

The Training Centres were established at all main coalfields where there was a labour shortage and were sited at either disused pits or at production pits where a training area could be segregated. The eleven main centres had from 280 to 520 places each, and by the end of April 1944 all the appointed Coalmining Training Centres were open, and an agreement was made with the Chislet Colliery company in Kent to cover training in that area.

By the end of October 1944, 45,800 ballotees, optants and volunteers had entered centres, of whom 1,800 failed to complete the course. Having completed the initial stage 'A' training, the trainee would then be posted by direction to the working colliery for continuing employment, where the next phase of training known as stage B, normally of two weeks' duration, would be given by the employer under the control of the Ministry of Fuel and Power.

In South Wales special conditions applied which required further training for a fortnight, before being employed on work below ground, and for the period of at least four weeks after starting regular underground work, they would come under the personal supervision of an experienced miner. Also it was necessary to complete at least four months' underground experience before working at the coal face.

In addition arrangements were made to send trainees to the existing scheme operated for the North Staffordshire Colliery Owners by the Local Education Authority at the North Staffordshire Technical College and the Kemball Pit. The question of establishing one or two additional centres was still under consideration at that time. Easington colliery was also used for training, although not one of the officially designated centres, probably acting as an auxiliary establishment for nearby

Horden.

With the end of the European War in May 1945, the ballot scheme was discontinued, but all ballotees, optants and volunteers would have to remain in the industry until a suitable release scheme could be implemented. Training was now only required for optants and volunteers, but after May most of the centres closed down and by the end of that year only three centres remained open at Birley, Oakdale and Muircockhall, with the continuation of training at the North Staffordshire Technical College at Stoke-on-Trent. Chislet Colliery Centre in Kent had also ceased training at the beginning of the year.

With the cessation of the ballot and the end of hostilities in Europe, the labour force in the industry began rapidly to decrease and arrangements were made for the block release under Class 'B' of 1,000 miners from the Army. However, this proved unsatisfactory as they would become subject to 'directions'.

In August it was agreed that Service Departments would arrange for special release from the forces of all miners accepted for re-employment by individual collieries.

On 29 November 1945, the Ministry of Labour announced in Parliament the basis on which ballotees, optants and volunteers who had entered coalmining employment in place of service in the armed forces would be entitled to apply for release from the industry. The basis for release would be similar to that of Class 'A' from the army.

Facts taken from PRO:LAB 8/734 and CAB 102/399

Message from the Minister of Labour and National Service to all Trainees entering Coal Mining Training Centres

It is the intention of the Government to provide the young people who are being directed into the coal mining industry with the best possible means of occupying their leisure time. All work and no play is good for nobody and there are very few who do not appreciate a game of football or cricket, a dance or a good film. Some colliery villages provide these facilities, but many do not, and a real effort will be made to remedy these deficiencies.

But recreation is not everything. There are many of you who have made up your minds what your future careers are going to be. Some of you have already started on a course of study leading to the profession or occupation of your choice and are wondering how you can continue your studies whilst you are employed in the mines. Others would like to study some other subjects, such as

Region	Colliery	Owner	Shaft/s Sunk	Employees Under-ground	Surface	Seams Worked	Closed
Scotland	Muircockhall (Fife)	Ness, Henry & Co. Ltd.	-	27	6	Three Feet, Ell, Fourteen Feet, Six Feet, Cairncubie & Upper & Lower Eight Feet	Dec 1944
Northern	Old Morrison (Durham)	Holmside & South Moor Collieries Ltd.	East 22 ft diam. downcast 269 yd 1923-25 West 22 ft diam. upcast 273 yd 1923-25	1441	281	Maudlin Hutton Low Main	Oct 1973
Northern	Horden (Durham)	Horden Collieries Ltd.	North & South 22 ft diam. downcast 142 yd 1900-04 East 17 ft diam. 1upcast 1908	2898	894	Low Main Hutton	Feb 1986
Northern	Cramlington Lamb (North'nd)	-	-	-	-	Training Centre	1939/1940
North Eastern	Askern Main (Yorkshire)	Askern Coal & Iron Co. Ltd. diam.	No.1 21~ ft diam. 566 yds 1911 No.2 21", ft 564 yd 1912	1170	354	Warren House Barnsley Seam	Dec 1991

Region	Colliery	Details			Seams	Shafts closed in
North Eastern	Prince of Wales (Yorkshire)	Pontefract No.1 18 ft diam. 662 yd Collieries Ltd. 1911-25 No.2 14 ft (Yorkshire) diam. 716 yd 1872-94 Prince of No.3 14 ft diam. 662 yd Wales 1872 Collieries	1543	454	Haigh Moor	Shafts closed in 1981, now a drift mine
North Eastern	Birley East (Yorkshire)	Sheffield Coal - Co. Ltd	30	50	Training Centre	1951
North Western	Newtown (Lancashire)	Manchester No.1 436 yd 2880 No.2 Collieries Ltd. 629 yd 1880 No.3 621 yd 1880	551	205	Doe, Victoria, Trencherbone	Apr 1961
North Midlands	Creswell (Derbyshire)	Bolsover No.1 18 ft diam. 445 yd Colliery Ltd 1894 No.2 18 ft diam. 445 yd 1896	1175	407	High Hazel	Sept 1991
Midlands	Haunchwood (Warwickshire)	Haunchwood 310 yd 1891-93 Collieries Ltd.	4	6	Pumping	Apr 1967
Wales	Oakdale (Monmouthshire)	Oakdale No.1 21 ft diam. 670 yd Navigation No.2 21 ft diam. 695 yd Collieries Ltd. 1908-10 Upper Rhas Las	1679	334	Big Vein, Meadow Vein,	Aug 1989
Midlands	Kemball (Staffordshire)*	Staffordshire - Coal & Iron Ltd.	360	165	Great Row Five Feet	1964
Southern	Chislet Kent	No information available. The colliery closed in July1969.				

*Part of Stafford No1, which also included Pender Bourne Bourne and Hem Heath

Kemball Colliery Training Centre was established in 1942 for training North Staffordshire boys who wanted to make a career in the mining industry. With the conscription of Bevin Boys in December 1943, Kemball became part of the Collie Training Centre network. The Collie closed in 1964 and continued as a Training Centre only.

Source: British Coal Corporation.

foreign languages or art. Some, I hope, will decide to remain permanently in coal mining and will wish to equip themselves for the higher posts in the industry. For all of you we want to make the best provision that we, and the education authorities, can.

As you know, you have been sent to the coal mines to help to produce more of the coal which is so urgently wanted to carry on the war. It would, therefore, be unreasonable to expect that you would be allowed time off during working hours to attend classes, unless, perhaps, you were studying mining with a view to making it your career, but evening classes in the towns cater for most of the popular needs and some of the more specialised subjects as well. The ideal would be that all those who desire to take classes in any particular subject should be placed at a colliery situated as near as possible to a centre at which such instruction could be obtained. This may not be possible, but an endeavour will be made to meet individual needs, once it is known what those needs are. In other words, if you have a wish to study for a particular trade, an attempt will be made, as far as circumstances permit, to place you at a colliery conveniently situated to a centre at which that trade is taught.

In order to make these arrangements it is necessary first to know immediately what you want and, if you wish to be considered, you should answer the questions below and return this form to your Centre Manager. You are, of course, under no obligation to complete the form unless you desire to take advantage of these arrangements, but if you do so and if you are given a reasonable opportunity of pursuing your studies, you will naturally be expected to make good use of it. So please let the Centre Manager know immediately what you want and we will do our best to provide it. If you would like advice before completing this form the Manager will endeavour to help you.

Signed ERNEST BEVIN
Minister of Labour and National Service

North Midlands Region	Creswell Colliery, Derbyshire
Midlands Region	*Haunchwood Colliery, Nuneaton, Warwickshire
North Western Region	*Newtown Colliery, Lancashire
North Eastern Region	Askern Main Colliery, Doncaster, Yorkshire
	Prince of Wales Colliery, Pontefract, Yorkshire
	Birley Colliery (East Pit), Woodhouse, Yorkshire
Northern Region	Morrison Colliery, Southmoor, Durham,
	*Horden Colliery, Durham Cramlington
	Lamb Colliery, Northumberland
Scotland	Muircockhall Colliery, Fife
Wales	Oakdale, Monmouthshire

*Opened by end of 1943.

Source: British Coal Corporation

Training Arrangements

Your Identification Number is No: Group: Class:

Training Period   Four weeks

Training Hours
> 8 15 a.m. to 4.15 p.m. Monday to Friday. Luncheon Interval, two groups, 11.30 - 12.30, after Lectures and P.T. 12.30 - 1.30 after underground and Surface Training. 8.15 a.m. to 12.15 p.m. Saturday.

Training
> Normal training will be apportioned as follows: Physical Training - one session per day. Lecture - one session per day. Underground work and surface work one session per day on alternate days, except last Monday in training, when full day will be spent underground. 1/2 hour allowed for mealtime underground. Trainee to bring packed meal and supply of water in Tin bottle, for this day only. See copy of time table exhibited in Lecture Room.

Leave
> While at the Centre leave can only be granted in exceptional circumstances of which proof will be required.

Rate of Wages
> A Notice is posted in the Hall and Lecture Rooms at the Centre showing rates of wages payable and deductions normally made each week.

Payment of Wages
> Wages are paid on Wednesday up to the previous Saturday. If you are a boarder you will receive an advance of £1. 4s.6d. on Wednesday in the first week of training, which will be recovered when settling-in grant or the first week's lodging allowances is paid on the following Wednesday. Other recoverable advances up to the maximum of three days earning may also be made in special circumstances to any trainee on application during the first week of training. Pay queries will be dealt with at the Accounts Office on Mondays and Thursdays at 10.30 - 12.30 and 2.30 - 4 p.m.

P.A.Y.E.
> You are advised to make sure that your code Number for tax purposes is correct in order to avoid queries about tax deduction. If you have not done so, hand form P.45 (tax form which should have been given to you by your previous employer) to the Reception Counter. If not in possession of this form a form P.I will be given to you for completion. This form should be left at the Accountant's Office as soon as possible. It is important that you should answer all the questions, as, otherwise, excessive deduction of tax may be made.

Baths

A charge of sixpence per week is made for the use of the Baths.

Buses

To and from Hostel. A charge of three shillings per week is made from Keresley Miner's Hostel to the Training Centre. This is paid by you to the Accountant after receipt of wages.

Unclaimed Wages and Queries other than Pay

Apply at the Centre Offices any day.

Kit

Your Kit consists of Safety Helmet, Overalls, Safety Boots, Gym shoes, Vests, Shorts, Padlock and Key. The Overalls, Gym shoes, Vest, Shorts, Padlock and Key must be returned at the end of the training period. Safety Helmet and Boots must be returned if you are permitted to terminate training prematurely. Gym shoes, Vest and Shorts may be worn only in the P.T. Class. LOST Kit must be paid for.

Time-keeping

Good Time-keeping is essential for efficient training.

Allocation

You have already been given an opportunity to express a preference for employment in a particular area, and if it were possible to do so that preference has been observed in allocating you to this Centre. Trainees are usually placed in the Region in which they are trained, or in accordance with special arrangements made by the Ministry of Fuel and Power by whom all allocations to work in collieries are made. Requests to be placed in other Regions cannot, therefore, be entertained, but if you wish to be placed in a particular pit or district in this Region you should state your circumstances to the Placing Officer during the allocation panel. No guarantee can, however, be given that it will be possible to arrange for you to go to the pit or district of your choice.

Allocation Panel

Representatives of the Ministry of Fuel and Power attend the Centre of Wednesday afternoon to interview Trainees in their second week of training, when the allocations to the various pits are made.

General Enquiries

If in doubt on any point ask at the Centre Office.

Correspondence

All correspondence by post should be addressed:
The Manager,
Government Training Centre,
The Tunnel Pit
Nuneaton
Warwickshire

Similar instructions were issued at other Training Centres.

Weekly Rates of Pay During Training

Age	s.	d.
17	39	6
17½	41	6
18	44	-
18½	46	-
19	48	-
19½	50	6
20	53	-
20½	55	-
21	78	-

Weekly Employment Rates after Training

Age	Underground		Surface	
	s.	d.	s.	d.
17	45	-	39	6
17½	48	6	41	6
18	52	-	44	-
18½	54	-	46	-
19	56	-	48	-
19½	58	-	50	6
20	60	-	53	-
20½	62	-	55	-
21	83	-	78	-

Courses and Training

	Course	Duration
Stage 'A'	All 'Bevin Boy' entrants	4 weeks
Stage 'B'	All 'Bevin Boy' entrants	2 weeks
Course A	Instructors - Electricians and Mechanics	1 week
Course B	Trainees 18-25 in Electrical and Engineering	26 weeks
Course C1	Instructors - Machine Operators	1 week
Course C2	Instructors - Under Officials handling of Modem Machinery	1 week

Introduced in 1945:

Course B(E)	Trainees - Electrical Engineering	6 weeks
Course B(M)	Trainees - Mechanical Engineering	16 weeks

Safely Rules for new entrants to coal mines. Notice E.D.L. 94

(1)   Before going underground in a safety lamp mine search your clothes for matches or forbidden articles.

(2)   When riding in the cage hold on to the handrail and do not interfere with the gates.

(3)   Behave in an orderly manner and observe instructions given by the colliery officials.

(4)   Take care of your lamp.

(5)   Walk at a safe distance behind or in front of moving tubs and keep on the outside of curves.

(6)   Do not pass across the shaft bottom or through a fence.

(7)   Keep behind tubs when taking them down a gradient.

(8)   Do not place your hands and elbows between tubs - other tubs may bump in behind and break your wrist or arm.

(9)   Avoid loose clothing or scarves with loose ends which may be gripped by moving machinery, ropes or chains.

(10) Do not ride on ponies, nor on tubs unless authorised and instructed to do so.

(11) Do not couple or uncouple tubs in motion.

(12) Leave doors and brattice sheets exactly as you found them before passing through.

(13) Make yourself familiar with the codes of haulage signals in use.

(14) Keep your place of work tidy and free from obstruction.

(15) Never oil or grease machinery whilst in action.

(16) Always use the safety devices provided.

(17) Report at once any damage to safety devices or machinery fencing.

(18) Do not interfere with electrical or other apparatus.

(19) Regulations are made for your safety - observe them.

(20) Small injuries if neglected may turn septic - report all injuries and have them properly dressed.

(21) Keep yourself fit and alert.

LAB 8/734

Facts and figures taken from PRO: CAB 102/399 British Coal Corporation

Doncaster Amalgamated Collieries Ltd.   **S.D. Form 4.**

REVISED SAFETY INSTRUCTIONS TO BOYS. CARD 1.

SURFACE INSTRUCTIONS

I HAVE BEEN WARNED.

1. To take special care before attempting to cross any railway lines or sidings.
2. Of the dangers of crawling under wagons.
3. Of the care necessary when working near the delivery end of picking belts.
4. Of the dangers when working near revolving shafts.
5. Of the dangers when working near the machinery driving picking belts and screens.
6. Not to ride or attempt to cross picking belts whilst the belts are in motion.
7. Of the dangers of removing guards and fences whilst the machinery is in motion.
8. Of the dangers of wearing unsuitable clothing, e.g. loose or torn clothing and scarves etc.
9. Not to interfere with anything unconnected with my job. This applies especially to Electrical and Compressed Air Machinery.
10. Not to interfere with Notices, but to read and make myself familiar with all notices when posted and comply with them.
11. Not to leave my working place without permission.
12. To read and comply with C.M.A. Abstract, M & Q Form 68, a copy of which I have received.

Doncaster Amalgamated Collieries Ltd. **S.D. Form 4.**

REVISED SAFETY INSTRUCTIONS TO BOYS. CARD I.
GENERAL INSTRUCTIONS.

I HAVE BEEN WARNED.

1. To always use the proper footpaths and gangways when moving about the Surface and to behave in an orderly manner.

2. To search myself for cigarettes, matches, petrol lighters, flash lamps and other prohibited articles, before approaching the shaft.

3. To examine my lamp before leaving the lamp cabin, to take great care of and keep my lamp burning, and never to leave it any distance.

4. Not to pass across the shaft bottom or through a fence.

5. Not to enter or leave the cage without permission of the Onsetter or Banksman and, to hold on to my lamp and the cage hand rail and to prevent anything belonging to me falling down the shaft.

6. To see the Deputy for instructions and to have my lamp tested before going to my working place.

7. Not to walk in the tub road or pass on the inside of turns around which ropes may be running.

8. To leave doors exactly as they were before passing through them, and if ropes are running, to pass through with the rope.

9. Not to interfere with anything unconnected with my job, especially Electrical Machinery or Apparatus, and Shaft signals.

10. Not to ride on tubs, clips, ropes, or ponies, or get on or off manhauler cars whilst in motion.

II. To keep a safe distance in front or behind moving tubs, and not pass through a set that is in motion or likely to move.

12. Not to mark or interfere with Notices, but to read and make myself familiar with all notices when posted and comply with them.

13. Not to give signals unless familiar with the system and code in use.

14. Not to leave my working place without permission.

15. To take care of and to wear my helmet at all times and to wear safety boots and suitable clothing, and to report any accident however slight.

16. To read and comply with C.M.A. Abstract, M & Q Form 70, a copy of which I have received.

REVISED SAFETY INSTRUCTIONS TO BOYS - CARD 2.
MECHANICAL HAULAGE

I HAVE BEEN SHEWN HOW

1. To operate signals and use my station code and not to give starting signals when the rope has been stopped by some other person.

2. To carry Clips, and hang them on tub sides.

3. To push, couple, uncouple and locker tubs safely.

4. To conduct tubs round Pulleys.

5. To operate Juts or Squezees.

6. To clip, and unclip tubs, whilst the rope is stationary, and whilst in motion.

7. To keep sets of Tubs the proper distance apart.

8. To use the Safety Devices provided.

9. To use a hook for coupling and uncoupling.

10. To use the telephone in a proper manner.

I HAVE BEEN WARNED

1. To give signals distinctly and to always use my station signal and report immediately if signals are out of order.

2. To keep a clear road underfoot.

3. Against the dangers of a broken wrist or forearm when separating tubs, and trapped fingers over edge of tub. To keep Head and Arms from between tubs or buffers when coupling. Not to couple tubs in motion. To use only good lockers.

4. To keep a sharp look out for tubs bumping into the set being coupled.

5. To keep a sharp look out for the front tub escaping after a bump from another run (when squezees are used).

6. To keep one hand on the tub whilst coupling or clipping, and of the possibility of falling backwards when clipping and not to use faulty clips.

7. To unclip a safe distance from pulleys, sloughs, or stationary runs. To stop the rope for a tight clip. Not to leave an open clip on the rope. To unclip runs of tubs before attempting to re-rail them.

8. Of the dangers of close sets and to keep behind sets moving down gradients.

9. Of the penalties for not using the Safety devices provided.

10. To note the nearest refuge hole, keep it clear of obstructions and not to rest in dangerous places on the haulage road.

11. Not to leave tubs in such a position as will cause interference with the ventilation and to see that all doors and cloths are left in the proper position.

Doncaster Amalgamated Collieries Ltd. S.D.   **Form 4.**

REVISED SAFETY INSTRUCTIONS TO BOYS. CARD 3.
OVER TUB HAULAGE.

I HAVE BEEN SHEWN HOW

1. To attach a lashing chain to tubs and how to lash on whilst the rope is in motion.
2. To knock off whilst the rope is in motion.
3. To take twists or knots out of the chain.
4. To extend tubs before putting the back end chain on.
5. To remove a chain that is twisted round the rope.
6. To space the tubs the proper distance apart.
7. Accidents have occurred whilst engaged on this work.

I HAVE BEEN WARNED

1. That new chains or ropes will not slip easily while making the coupling.
2. To keep twists out of the chain and to knock off a chain that is twisting and recouple.
3. To keep my hands clear of the loose laps of chain while completing the lashing.
4. Not to use damaged chains or hooks, and to send them out of the pit.
5. To keep the rope in the centre of the tubs.
6. To make sure that all tub couplings are fully extended before securing back chain.
7. Of the possibility of loose ends of Clothing, Scarves, etc. being gripped by chain links.
8. That a chain sloughed by a fixed device must be removed at once, or the rope stopped.
9. Never to allow chains to drag on the floor.
10. To keep clear of slack rope at derailments.
11. To stop the rope and approach cautiously a run that is fast and that chains and links on tension might burst or fly off causing severe injury.
12. To only attempt to lift the rope back onto tubs when plenty of assistance is available, keeping my legs and feet clear.

Doncaster Amalgamated Collieries Ltd.　　　　**S.D. Form 4.**

REVISED SAFETY INSTRUCTIONS TO BOYS. CARD 4.
PONY HAULAGE

I HAVE BEEN SHEWN HOW

1. To approach a pony when in the stables.
2. To harness and unharness my pony.
3. To limber him up, or use Sling Gears.
4. To attach him to or detach him from tubs using a Cotter pin for limbers.
5. To pass through doors or cloths with pony and tub so as not to cause any interference with ventilation, and to report any damage that may be done.
6. To use the Safety Devices coupled to tubs such as Drags and to keep other devices such as blocks, dumplings and jack-catches in working order.
7. To lead my pony to and from the stables and to keep a safe distance behind other ponies being led.

I HAVE BEEN WARNED

1. To examine my pony and harness during the shift and report any sores, injury, loss of shoes or defective harness at once to the Deputy or Corporal, and again when taking the pony back to the stables.
2. To see that limbers are kept off the pony's hocks and that chains are not left hanging.
3. To stand from between the rails when attaching or detaching my Pony.
4. To uncouple Pony before attempting to lift a derailed tub on.
5. Of the penalties for not using Drags, etc.
6. To provide light, water and food for the pony and report a shortage.
7. To report when Pony catches roof, or sides, or any injury to Pony.
8. Not to leave Pony coupled to tubs, but to fasten him securely to a solid support, and locker up the run of tubs. 9. Not to ride on the pony or tubs.
10. Not to attempt to take my pony through a narrow opening.
11. Not to attempt to turn my Pony round between tubs or in a narrow roadway as the pony may knock out roof supports or bolt and cause injuries to me or himself.
12. To report immediately any damage to the track or safety devices to my Corporal or Deputy.

Doncaster Amalgamated Collieries Ltd.   **S.D. Form 4.**

REVISED SAFETY INSTRUCTIONS. CARD 5.
DRIVING ENGINES

I HAVE BEEN SHEWN HOW

1. How and where to hang my lamp safely.
2. To test out the signals on arrival at the engine and before starting.
3. To drive the various types of small haulage engines in use at this Colliery.
4. To make. sure that all fencing is securely fixed before starting the engine.
5. To blowout the flexible hose before coupling up and starting the engine.
6. To uncouple hose or switch off current and leave everything safe.
7. To use the various types of fire extinguishers installed.

I HAVE BEEN WARNED

1. To be sure of signals before starting Engines or Belts.
2. Not to reverse the belts until someone is on guard at the Tension end.
3. Not to leave the engine whilst the machinery is in motion.
4. Not to remove guards to oil or clean machinery whilst it is in motion.
5. Not to wear loose clothing which might be caught in the machinery.
6. To keep the engine house and vicinity clean and tidy.
7. Never to hesitate in reporting anything that may be a danger to myself or others to the official under whose charge I am working and not to be afraid of making suggestions at any time on this or any other subject which may lead to greater safety.

REVISED SAFETY INSTRUCTIONS. CARD 6.
GATE LOADERS AND CONVEYORS

I HAVE BEEN SHEWN HOW

1. To conduct tubs in a safe manner to the Gate Loader.
2. To hold tubs whilst being filled, and use the Safety Equipment provided for this purpose (Loader Gloves and Hooks).
3. To test signals before starting loaders or conveyors and to start and stop the loader and conveyor belts when receiving signals to do so, and not to leave running machinery.
4. To fasten the trailing cables or air hoses up in a safe place in the vicinity of the loader.
5. To clean up under and around the loader when it has stopped, and apply stone dust.
6. To operate the fire extinguisher provided and to keep the same hung up and clear of damage.
7. To operate the fire hydrant, to make sure that water is available at the commencement of the shift, run out hose, and how to use the jet when fighting fires.
8. To blowout uncoupled flexible hose before coupling same to a machine, and to uncouple and to leave everything safe.
9. To use, and where the hang the automatic firedamp detector and to keep it under observations for the whole shift. On any sign of gas being present to stop the machinery.

I HAVE BEEN WARNED.

1. That the machinery should not be run whilst guards are out of position and never to reverse the belts unless someone is on guard at the tension end.
2. To keep my hands from inside the guards and fencing, and not to oil or clean the machinery whilst it is in motion. Not to stand on belts whilst they are in motion.
3. To keep my hands from the tops of the tubs when pushing them under the Loader end.
4. To stop the Loader when a derailment occurs.
5. To use the Jutts and Lockers provided.
6. Never to leave the machinery running unattended.
7. To keep the Free Return Wheel clear of coal dust, timber, etc.
8. To keep clean and in proper working order Jack-catches or other devices installed for my safety.
9. To tackle a fire promptly and from the intake side.
10. To immediately report any damage to the machinery or electrical equipment.

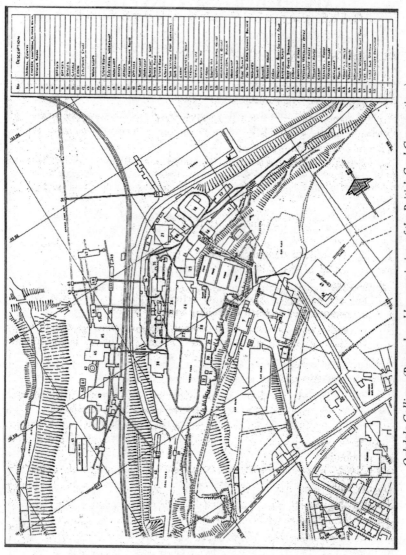

Oakdale Colliery. (Reproduced by permission of the British Coal Corporation.)

Morrison Pit, Annfield Plan, c. 1916.
(Reproduced by permission of Beamish, The North of England Open Air Museum,
County Durham.)

Harden Colliery c. 1910,
(Reproduced by permission of Beamish, The North of England Open Air Museum,
County Durham.)

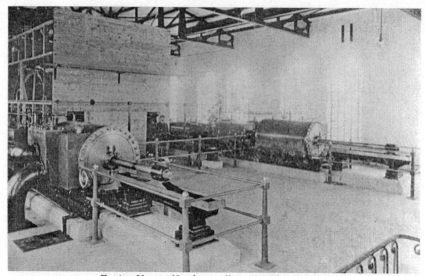

Engine House, Hordern colliery (winding engine)
(Reproduced by permission of Beamish, The North of England Open Air Museum,
County Durham.)

Cramlington Lamb Colliery, 1934
(Photo: J. Tuck)

Askern Main Colliery post-1947.
(Reproduced by permission of the British Coal Corporation.)

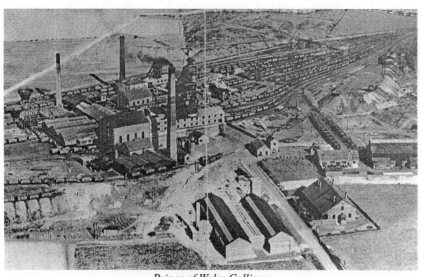

Prince of Wales Colliery
(Reproduced by permission of Pontefract Museum)

Birley (East) Colliery, date unknown.
(Reproduced by permission of the British Coal Corporation.)

Newton Colliery, c.1926
(Reproduced by permission of Salford Mining Museum

Haunchwood Colliery, 1946. (Reproduced by permission of the British Coal Corporation.)

67

Cresswell Colliery, 1950. The group of people are awaiting news after the disastrous underground fire, from which the bodies of 80 miners were recovered on 26th September 1950. (Photo: Denis Thorpe. Manchester Guardian. *Reproduced by permission of Salford Mining Museum.)*

Kemball Colliery, c. 1961
(Reproduced by permission of the British Coal Corporation.)

Oakdale Colliery; 1976,
(Reproduced by permission of the British Coal Corporation.)

Chislet Colliery, post-1947
(Reproduced by permission of the British Coal Corporation.)

A group of Bevin Boys at Birley East Colliery, 1944
(Photo courtesy of S. Payne)

A group of Bevin Boys training at Oakdale Colliery, 1944

A group of Bevin Boys at Morrison Colliery, 1944
(Photo courtesy of J. Cook)

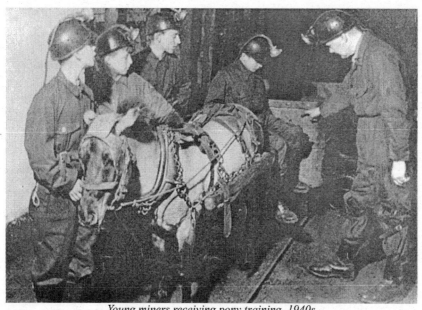

Young miners receiving pony training, 1940s
(Reproduced by permission of J. Tuck)

6

Coal, Coke and Anthracite

It was unlikely that a Bevin Boy would have been employed to work on the surface, as this would normally be filled by miners unfit for underground work. Bevin Boys had to have a medical category of A1, but if subsequently found to be below this standard, a transfer would most likely result to a branch of the forces or even an absolute discharge.

A colliery was always distinguished by the steel lattice head-frames which housed the giant wheels and winding gear above the shafts, together with the nearby mountainous slag heaps scattered around the countryside.

A shaft would contain a pair of cages often double-decked, one being located at the pit bottom and the other on the surface, alternating when operated by the engineman in the winding house. These were powered by steam in most cases with a few being electrically driven in the larger collieries. Against the sides of the shaft were housed electric cables and water pipes for use underground, but in some mines water had to be pumped out where flooding occurred.

Collieries would generally have more than one shaft which, apart from increasing output to the surface, acted as a ventilating system known as downcast and upcast shafts. As the description implies, air would be pumped down one shaft and extracted from the other, with some of the larger closely connected collieries having a common ventilating system servicing more than one pit.

Where only one working shaft existed with no means of ventilation, an additional smaller shaft, not designed to carry tubs or miners, would be sunk into the mine at a distance from the main shaft, with a fan house situated for circulating and extracting spent air.

Processing of coal varied in different regions, determined by the type of coal mined, as to suitability for use as industrial steam coal, anthracite, domestic blends or for conversion into coke.

Upon reaching the surface the 10-cwt tubs or larger high-sided one ton would be checked, weighed and then conveyed and discharged onto shaker screens in the screening house for grading and sizing, a very noisy operation for anyone working in this area.

A typical example would involve the extraction of coal of less than 1½ in. which would be washed, cleaned and, if suitable for conversion to coke, transferred to the coke ovens. Larger sizes up to 8 in. were similarly treated and above this size probably cleaned by hand, with all the processed coal finally taken to large storage areas to await loading and despatch by rail, or in certain areas by barge on the inland canals. Collieries had their own railway sidings to accommodate their own loco-motives for shunting and rolling stock prior to rail nationalisation in 1948. Loaded wagons in the sidings would await transfer to various parts of the country carrying industrial or domestic coal, whilst empty wagons were systematically moved to coal-loading hoppers for filling and weighing. Dust from the shaker screens and cleaning plant could be pulverised and used as fuel for firing the boilers in the coke ovens or other parts of the colliery where heat was needed. However, invariably the dust waste from coal and rock was conveyed in aerial ropeway buckets and dis-charged some distance away, thus forming unsightly slag heaps upon the landscape.

A coal mine does not just consist of pithead winding gear, shafts, or 'bank' as it is known, with chimneys, railway sidings and slag heaps, but several other build-ings and workshops would be scattered around the colliery site. On the mechanical and electrical side there were buildings to house a power and compressor station, fan house, work and repair shops for welding, mechanical and tub repairs, stores, storage bunkers, weigh house, saw mill, stables and a hay store for the horses and ponies, together with a blacksmith's shop.

In another part of the colliery, office buildings, medical first aid, canteen and pithead bath facilities would be found.

Pithead baths consisted of a clean and dirty side, with showers between. The object being that when arriving for a shift, entry would be made from the clean side where clothing would be left in a locker. Moving straight to the dirty side taking your water bottle, snap tin, soap and towel, of which the latter two would be left in a similar locker where the change was made into working clothes. At the finish of a shift the process would be reversed with a shower taken between.

The whole area of the baths would be a surround of white tiles, a total contrast from the black environment experienced only minutes earlier. A rotating brush for boot cleaning was also installed as part of the equipment of the 362 pithead baths that were in existence during the time of the Bevin Boy, the war curtailing the building of further baths and facilities.

7

Dangers and Discomforts

The colliery to which one was posted invariably came under the same region as that of the initial training centre, where once again accommodation would either be in a miners' hostel or local lodgings.

After a further two weeks' training Stage 'B' work would start in earnest, usually at the colliery where this second phase of training was completed, although in a few cases allocation might be made to another colliery owned by the same company, being at that time under private ownership prior to nationalisation.

Before attempting to go underground it was necessary to obtain from the check office a numbered disc serving as a personal identification, which if not returned at the end of the shift, would indicate that the miner was still below ground and thus warrant further investigation.

The second important item was the miner's safety lamp which would be collected and checked from the lamp house. At most collieries the lamp number would correspond with that of the check number, but a few operated an additional check system for the issue of lamps, which varied according to suitability for conditions underground. Battery-type lamps were either a Concordia hand lamp or the lamp attached to the hard hat, with the battery being strapped to the waist belt making a total weight of 6 lb.

Flame Safety Lamps, known as the Protector lamp, were the other common type generally issued to the miners. A relighter and automatic gas detector type issued to Deputies and shot firers was a statutory requirement. Another lamp, known as the Ringrose Miner's Lamp, was a combination of the two flame safety lamps. These lamps, apart from providing illumination, were capable of detecting and measuring the percentage of methane, marsh or firedamp gas, a reading of 4 to 5 percent indicating the danger of explosion.

In the queue before entering the cage, a contraband check for any cigarettes, matches or lighters would be conducted in the form of a body search by the Banksman, who was responsible for the loading, unloading, control of the gates and signalling for the winding house to lower or raise the cage.

No Bevin Boy will ever forget his first descent or initiation drop down the pit shaft during training, and it is not surprising that the full force of gravity would naturally cause considerable pressure on the ear drums, nose and stomach. During the course of a descent, old previously worked levels might be passed on the way down to the pit bottom, whereupon the miner would emerge from the cage into a well-lit tunnel or gallery, usually faced with white-washed bricks and supported by timber and semi-circular arched girders. This area consisted of haulage roads leading into the mine, with rail tracks laid on the ground for conveying tubs.

Various methods of mechanical haulage were used and most Bevin Boys worked at some stage with this operation. Standard systems would involve the use of clips, known as 'clamping', for attachment to the front and rear of a 'journey' or number of tubs coupled to a moving steel rope running at ground level between the tracks. Another similar method involved the use of chains 'lashing' attached to overhead ropes. The 'Main and Tail' haulage employed the use of ropes for direct attachment to the tubs without clips or chains. Along the roof or side of the roadway would run two exposed low voltage electric wires which, by shorting together, would ring a bell where the engineman operated the rope haulage engine and by a system of bell signalling codes would indicate whether to start or stop the cables.

Where this method of haulage was not available, collieries employed the use of horses or pit ponies for the movement of the tubs. The horse or pony was always a favourite with the miners, becoming quite attached to their handlers, especially if any tit-bits were forthcoming from their snap tins and a very useful friend in the event of a faulty miner's lamp, when the pony would by instinct always know and lead the way back to the pit bottom in total darkness. These animals were stabled below ground and only brought to the surface for a rest during the annual one week's holiday, when they were again stabled for a couple of days to allow gradual adjustment to daylight from a state of blindness before being released into the fields.

Miners once below ground would report to the Overman's Office, an Overman having the role of a management supervisor in charge of a district, and it was always good policy to keep on the right side of them to avoid being allocated to one of the less popular jobs. This could also apply to the District Fireman or Deputy, who had equal powers of authority and on occasion would conduct contraband searches. No machinery would be started up until the oncoming shift were positioned at their work station, which could take some time covering the distance from the pit bottom as often tunnels extended for several miles. Where no manhauler cars were installed, the riding in tubs was used as a form of transport to convey miners into the mine, although this practice was not generally permitted, the alternative being to cover the distances on foot. This in itself could be quite exhausting at the start or finish of a shift, in conditions of uneven terrain in restricted spaces with low ceilings, carrying a miner's lamp in one hand with a snap tin and flask of water in the other.

The large main tunnel would eventually lead into smaller unlit tunnels or galleries during which a number of doors or brattice sheets would be encountered. These were placed to regulate the ventilation and prevent the flow of air from entering side tunnels and thus reduce the efficiency of air from areas where it was needed.

These smaller tunnels cut through coal or bare rock and, as cutting into the coal face advanced, extracted rock or coal had to be cleared, involving much use of the pick and shovel, and the area made secure with supports to the sides and roof. A fault or fractured seam out of alignment also presented additional problems which had to be overcome in order to continue production. It is not the intention to go into the technical detail of the various types of electrical or air compressor operated machinery, of which only a brief mention is made.

Many Bevin Boys worked alongside experienced colliers in the more skilled jobs of operating the various types of coal-cutting machines. For example, scraper chains a type of conveyor which cut and scraped against the coal by means of an endless chain of which the tension end had to be kept clear of slack, as the coal moved away from the coal face to the main conveyor belt. Other jobs would involve the use of the Tadger, a heavy electric drill for drilling holes for the placing of explosive charges, and work on conveyors, loaders and haulage engines. Originally it was suggested that they would not work at the coal face, but in any event was not compulsory for anyone under the age of twenty-one years, but this rule was not necessarily adhered to. The constant flow of coal from the face would be sprayed with jets of water in order to reduce the levels of dust and eliminate the risk of explosion, as well as cooling the drills. Conveyor belts, which might extend from more than one tunnel and coal face, would transfer the coal to a main loader or tip end where empty tubs would be filled ready for transportation to the pit bottom.

The continuous handling and movement of tubs by any method was bound to cause a risk of injury to the hands and fingers, with the possibility of more serious injury by being dragged along the ground or even crushed between tubs, as happened in each case involving the death of a Bevin Boy.

The system of "*data putting*" meant that a token with a letter or number marked on it would be placed on the loaded tub, which upon reaching the surface would be checked, weighed and tipped, thus crediting a bonus payment for each token earned. In South Wales a chalk mark sufficed as a token. Coal getting is a term which applied to those involved in the extraction of coal from the seam, who were known as colliers. During the course of a shift, the cages were in constant use for hauling tubs to the surface, a loading area in which extreme caution had to be taken, and at a Durham colliery a Bevin Boy was killed when struck by a descending cage.

The discomforts and disadvantages were numerous in the coalmining industry, miners working under conditions that were either hot, especially in deep mines, or cold, wet, draughty and smelly amongst dirt, dust and the constant noise of machinery. The absence of toilets would mean having to answer the call of nature more or less on the spot, as disappearing into a crevice was not encouraged in case of pockets of methane or marsh gas, and the use of tubs was not desirable and would most certainly invite uncomplimentary remarks from fellow miners, as bad language was fairly prominent in any event. Rats and mice were also unpleasant visitors, probably attracted by the straw which had been brought down for the stables, and they would not hesitate in seizing any opportunity of stealing food and sandwiches if snap tins were not used.

The dangers of working in a coal mine are known to be vast, which accounts for the many safety rules and regulations laid down by the Mines Safety Act. Accidents are inevitable in this type of industry, with the added hazards of rock falls caused by unstable ground or collapsing roofs, with the ever present fear of the risk of fire and explosion where gas is present. Those working in confined spaces might suffer with a condition known as "Housemaid's Knee", or beat knee, a chronic inflammatory swelling of the knee cap, caused as a result of prolonged kneeling despite the use of knee pads. The derailing of tubs was another common cause of injury, together with cuts and bruises accumulated during the course of a working day, and Bevin Boys were no exception to these hazards as two out of a total of twenty-one men were killed in an explosion at the Louisa and Old Morrison Colliery in Durham on 22 August 1947.

The loading of tubs into the cages would cease when miners made ready for return to the surface, under the control of the Onsetter who was responsible for loading and unloading below ground and by means of a bell signal. He would be in communication with the Banksman and Engineman in the winding house to raise the cage.

Upon returning to the surface, the safety lamp would be returned to the lamp house in exchange for the metal disc which was returned to the check office, although this was not always done. In spite of feeling tired, exhausted and thoroughly dirty, a mad rush would be made for the pithead baths if the colliery had these facilities; otherwise it would mean taking a bath at the hostel or lodgings, quite possibly involving a bus journey. Winter months would limit the hours of daylight to one or two hours after working a shift in the pit, which all added to a dismal and depressing environment.

The Bevin Boy often became the subject of practical pranks being played by the regular miners, which invariably when taken in good part went a long way to being accepted. However, sometimes a joke could misfire and this story is a true one.

A Bevin Boy was accompanying a shot firer who had just set about a dozen charges, and they had both retreated to their firing point to turn the plunger on the hand-operated generator. Expecting a rather large explosion which did not occur, the shot firer instructed the Bevin Boy to stay put, whilst he returned to the coal face to check the connections, and then returned once again to the firing point. After a second attempt at detonating the collier shouted, 'They still won't blow, must be damp,' to which the Bevin Boy replied, 'I know, I tried it twice while you were gone.'

Statistics show that one in four underground or surface workers were either killed or injured during 1943. In a five and a half year period, 6,000 men in South Wales alone suffered from silicosis or pneumoconiosis and 2,262 men were certified with the eye disease know as nystagmus throughout the industry during the first six months of 1945. Pneumoconiosis and progressive massive fibrosis (P.M.F) both result from the exposure to coal dust, often leading to emphysema. Again in South Wales between 1931 and July 1948, 19,000 men were certified under the Workman's Compensation Act. All were suspended from further work in the mining industry. In 1943, 713 miners were killed in pit accidents and in 1945, 550 were killed; 2,353 suffered from serious injuries during that period. No workman's compensation was paid other than burial expenses from the Government.

Source: D. Agnew
Colliery Guardian

Serious coalmine accidents involving loss of life from March 1945 to September 1947

4 March 1945 at Manvers Main Colliery in South Yorkshire, an explosion occurred during the early hours of the night shift in No. 1 Pit Meltonfield Seam. The cause was due to fire damp ignited by an electronic flash or spark from a short circuit in the trailing cable feeding the Joy Loader. Five deaths resulted through shock of burns, multiple crushing, fractures of and injuries to cranium, thorax and chest.

9 *December 1946* at Harrington No. 10 Colliery in Cumberland, an explosion occurred just after 7.00 a.m. on the early shift in No. 2 district. The cause was due to fire damp probably ignited by an electric cap lamp. Fifteen were killed and one injured.

10 January 1947 at Burngrange Nos. 1 & 2 in Midlothian, an explosion occurred at 8.00 p.m. which originated at the face of No. 4 level. The cause was due to an open acetylene cap lamp which ignited fire damp. Fifteen were killed, of which one died of a fractured skull and fourteen from carbon monoxide poisoning. There was a series of explosions.

7 *May 1947* at Barnsley Main Colliery in South Yorkshire, an explosion occurred at 12.15 p.m. during the day or filling shift. The explosion near the top end of No. 3 right face was caused by a trailing cable which ignited fire damp. Nine were killed and twenty injured.

22 August 1947 at Louisa and Morrison Old Colliery in Durham an explosion occurred at 11.55 p.m. during the night shift in the East Face. The cause was due to the striking of a Lucifer match which ignited fire damp. Twenty-one were killed and three injured.

9 *September 1947* at Ingham Colliery in Yorkshire, an explosion occurred at 11.15 p.m. during the night shift in No. 2 South District of the Wheatley Lime Seam. The cause was due to fire damp ignited by attempting to relight a Prestwich Type 6 safety lamp No. 9, which had probably been opened by cutting the lead rivet lock in an attempt to operate the relighting device. Twelve were killed and one injured.

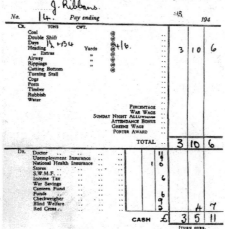

Pay Docket dated 24 March 1945 of a Bevin Boy employed at the Werfa Dare Colliery in South Wales. (J. Ribbans.)

The Concordia electric hand lamp,
type K.G. 240.

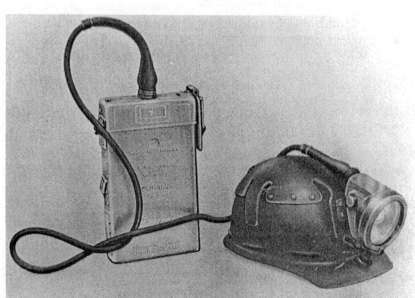

The Concordia cap lamp, type C.L. 3/M. The battery is carried behind the wearer's
back held by a waist strap, while the cable passes upwards and over the hard hat.

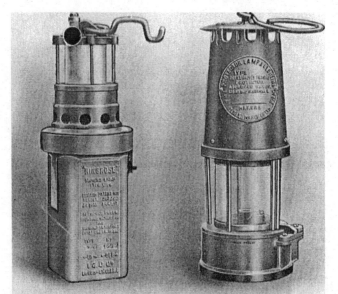

The Ringrose Gas Detector, C.H. 4 type   The Protector Safety lamp.
Both carried by workmen.

The Protector Officla's lamp (Relighter type),

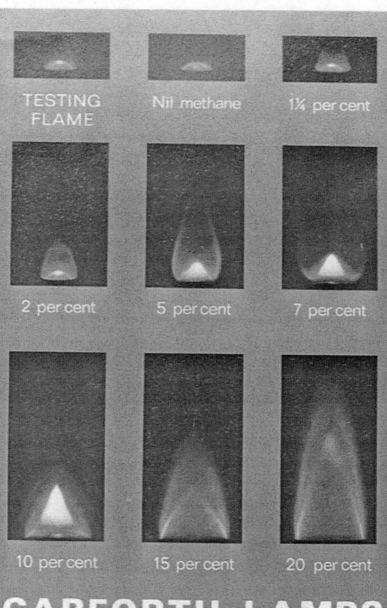

8

Absenteeism

Absenteeism amongst Bevin Boys was only to be expected, forced as they were into an occupation against their will. Right from the start, even during the initial four-week training period, a ten minute late arrival attending the 8.00 a.m. lecture class would make the individual or individuals liable to forfeit a day's pay. This situation would then trigger off an attitude of reluctance to remain with the class for the remainder of that particular day, thereby creating a situation where one would walk out and spend the rest of the day absconding from class.

The question of absenteeism became more apparent towards the end of 1944, thus the cause for concern arose as extracts from the letter of 30 January 1945 from the Ministry of Fuel and Power to the National Conciliation Board for the Coal Mining Industry shows.

With regard to your request for particulars of absenteeism of Bevin Boys, the following table shows the comparison between absenteeism by Bevin Boys and by other wage-earners in England and Wales during the week ended 25th November 1944.

	Bevin Boys		Other workers	
	Vol. %	Invol. %	Vol. %	Invol. %
At the face	13.42	14.49	6.93	10.77
Elsewhere below ground	12.89	14.78	5.71	9.20
On the surface	9.03	10.77	3.38	6.73
Overall	13.76	14.53	5.62	9.13

The figure for voluntary absenteeism of Bevin Boys may be inflated by the fact that it will include the shifts lost by trainees who have simply disappeared but who are still on colliery books. If 5% of the Bevin Boys come within this category, then the voluntary absenteeism percentage for England and Wales would fall to 8.2%, i.e. about 45% greater than the corresponding figure for other workers. It is significant that the involuntary absenteeism for Bevin Boys is 60% above the figures for other workers. Probably the best way of summing up of figures is to say that Bevin Boys absenteeism is half as much again as the total figure for other workers.

Information for Bevin Boys in Scotland has not been collected separately for those employed at the face and elsewhere.

Absenteeism overall was 11.39% voluntary and 10.07% involuntary, as compared with 4.69% and 4.97% respectively for other workers. The Scottish figures should not be compared with those given for England and Wales because they are at present compiled on a different basis. A separate comparison of Bevin Boys with other workers can, however, be made, and this gives a result of three quarters as much again as the total for other workers.

Throughout the regions the Ministry of Fuel and Power set up various Panels and Investigating Officers to deal with cases of absenteeism and lateness for work. Refusal to comply with the laid down procedures would inevitably lead to prosecution. In the Controller General's Ministry of Fuel and Power letter dated 30 January 1945, it stated that figures showed that the Bevin Boys' absenteeism was half as much again as the total figure for other workers; Bevin Boys only accounted for 16,000 out of a total number of 700,000 workmen employed, so that the effect of the increase of absenteeism on the part of Bevin Boys only accounted for 0.17 per cent; Also that the work performed by Bevin Boys was not as good as that of the boys normally recruited to the industry. It was thought that Bevin Boys were looking forward to getting out of the industry, so that naturally their interest would not be the same as those who were willing to remain in the industry for the rest of their lives.

In 1938 about 227,000,000 tons of coal had been produced when 781,700 men were employed. At the moment the number of persons employed 700,200 or a reduction of 71,000 persons, which would account for 5 to 6 million tons drop in output. However, other factors contributed to the fall in output as owners had not been working the most prolific seams, and the breakdown of machinery which had increased by approximately 50 per cent.

Another factor was that of the age level whereby 100,000 in the industry were over 55, a five-year increase on the average age due to the war years.

The psychological effect of the introduction of Bevin Boys on the rest of the workers in the pit meant that they were not replacing the man power which had been lost. The miners, therefore, in the armed forces should be released.

In 1944 there had been 3,000 more men employed, but the output per person had gone down to 259 tons. However, it was thought that absenteeism in South Wales was higher in the mines than in other industries and that they could make up the difference between 197,000,000 and 227,000,000 tons, if they were able to deal with the various causes contributing to loss of output.

The figures show the causes of loss of output.

Causes of Loss of output	1st Quarter 1944	1st Quarter 1945	Difference
Recognised holidays	480,000	982,000	502,9000
Disputes	2,032,900	343,100	1,689,800
Accidents, machinery Breakdowns & repairs	389,100	495,900	106,800
Rail transport Difficulties	420,400	603,600	183,200
Other causes	180,100	325,400	145,300
Total	3,502,500	2,750,900	˙751,600

The increase on account of recognised holidays was due to the fact that in the 1944 period Good Friday was included.

It was felt that there were insufficient numbers of men at the face to feed the men out-bye. This was reckoned in South Wales to account for 3,000,000 tons or four per cent, compared with two and a half per cent for the country generally. Absenteeism, however, was a principle cause for loss of production when, despite the measures taken by pit committees and courts, the attitude was one of not caring, and fining the culprits too much would only result in ultimate loss of output.

Morale was further affected by the fact that the Government would not issue travel passes and the men to have leave four days before the holiday started and two after it had finished, which was bound to have an effect on the youngsters in the hostels.

The question of men who were working five or six days week after week, apart from the abnormal shift hours, were not in a position to keep it up. A loss of one day out of six would represent sixteen per cent absenteeism.

In a report in the Government publication entitled 'Coal', on the subject of 'The Mineworker', it was said that the Bevin Boy ballotee had a record of bad attendance and discipline, and their influence was not good over the young labour in the mines. Absenteeism among ballotees and optants was double that among regular miners. Much absence was caused by sickness or accidents among these newcomers to a heavy industry. There were many discharges every year for incorrigibility, indiscipline and absenteeism, highest among young workers generally. The report goes on to say that the Essential Work Order and the application of direction, unavoidable as they must both be judged to have been, proved an evil not only from the standpoint of the men themselves but also from that of the industry. There is an old view that compulsory labour is inefficient because it is unwilling, borne out by the record of directed labour in the coal industry during the war, not withstanding the good service rendered by many directed men.

British Coal Corporation
Facts and figures taken from PRO: COAL 11/101
H.M.S.O 'Coal'.

Absence from Work (both voluntary and involuntary)		
	Overall rate %	At coal face %
1941	9.0	11.2
1942	10.4	12.8
1943	12.1	14.7
1944	13.3	15.9
1945 (1st Quarter)	15.8	18.2

1.0. Form No.1

Ministry of Fuel and Power
Region
Date

To:-
Dear Sir,
I have received information from your employers alleging that you have been absent from work without reasonable excuse/that you have been persistently late for work.

on   occasions during the past   weeks.
I am accordingly to request you to attend for interview
at
on   at
when your case will be heard either by the Panel or by the Investigating Officer.

If you agree to your case being heard in your absence, you should complete the attached form and return it to me using the enclosed label which need not be stamped.

Regional Investigation Officer

1.0. Form No.3

Special Voluntary Arrangements for dealing with Employers Reports on absenteeism and lateness.

I acknowledge having received from the Regional Investigation Officer notification that I have been absent from work/late in presenting myself for work on the following dates.

I agree that I should be interviewed by the Regional Investigation Officer assisted by representatives of the management of the Colliery at which I am employed and of my Trade Union and that in the absence of representatives of the management or the Trade Union, my case shall be dealt with by the Regional Investigation Officer.

I voluntarily agree to be fined if the Regional Investigation Officer so directs, a sum not exceeding One Pound (£1) and that this amount shall be deducted by my employer from the first week's wages accruing to me after the date of the recommendation of the Regional Investigation Officer. I further agree that the amount of the said fine shall be paid to a charity chosen by my Trade Union, unless after expiry of a period of four weeks from the date of deduction, the Regional Investigation Officer is satisfied that I have not during that period been absent or been late without good and sufficient reason and (in his discretion) directs my employer to refund such amount to me.

I agree to accept any decision of the Regional Investigation Officer as final and binding.

Signature
Check Number
Colliery
Date

9

Productivity

The results for 1944 and 1945 in terms of additional or more highly skilled manpower provided for the coalmining industry were:

Men placed in employment						
Year	Ballotees	Volunteers	Optants	Ex H.M.F.	Conscientious Objectors	Total
1944	15,362	3,139	8,668	4,745	3	31,917
1945	5,534	1,475	6,989	1,906	38	15,943
Totals	20,896	4,614	15,657	6,651	41	47,859

The employment of Bevin Boys in the coalmines within the nine regions is detailed in the chart. It shows the total number of ballotees, volunteers and optants who were directed to colliery employment for Government Training Centres up to 7 April 1945. In addition, the chart shows the number of Bevin Boys who were upgraded to work at the coal face, and the number of regular underground workers who were upgraded to productive work at the coal face as a direct result of the introduction of Bevin Boys up to the end of March 1945.

At question time in the House of Commons in April 1948, the Minister of Fuel and Power was asked how many boys directed to the mines entered the coalmines after the institution of the ballot; and how many of those were engaged at the coal face; and what actual operations the others were engaged in.

Major Lloyd George replied:

The number of men who have completed training at Government Training Centres and have been directed to coalmining employment is about 43.500, of whom approximately one half have been directed as the result of the ballot. Some 6,500 are reported as being now employed at the coal face. The remainder are engaged on various classes of underground work, ancillary to actual coal getting, such as maintenance of haulage roads, attending to track points, attaching and detaching coal tubs and trams and controlling the movement of underground transport. A comparatively small number of them who had mechanical and electrical experience before entering the Government Training Centres are employed on electrical or mechanical maintenance and repair work underground. My Hon. Friend will appreciate that, quite apart from the tonnage produced by those actually working at the coal face, the introduction of these men into mines has been of great value in making possible the upgrading of some 11.000 miners to the coal face.

From the figures it will be seen that the ballot scheme did not, in 1944 or subsequently, give the hoped for 50,000 trainees. It gave 15,000 in 1944 and something over 20,000 altogether before compulsory direction of young men to underground mining was stopped on the cessation of fighting with Germany in May 1945. Not more than 6,000-7,000 ballotees ever went to the coal face but, as stressed by the Minister of Fuel and Power in a parliamentary reply, 11,000 miners were released for upgrading to coal face through introduction of 'Bevin Boys' on to haulage and other duties in and about the mines. Also the setting up of Training Centres, primarily to accommodate the ballotees, made possible the training (with consequent value to production) of volunteers, optants, ex-servicemen and conscientious objectors, who were going into mining - over 21,000 by the end of March 1945 - and provided the facilities for higher grade training, the need for which was being stimulated by the insertion of 'Bevin Boys' into the industry's labour hierarchy. On the other hand, it is easy to see that the additional workers brought into the industry by the use of the ballot system would - coming as they did from all areas and walks of life - usually have an intense aversion to work which had been steadily growing in unpopularity even with men and boys from mining areas and mining families. So it can be assumed that increase in output would not be proportionate to the new intake and that most of the ballotees would be anxious to leave the industry as soon as they could. But, at least, the use of the ballot scheme tided over the immediate manpower crisis of coalmining and coal production struggled through, without further drastic manpower expedients, to the end of the war.

In South Wales and Monmouthshire it was found that out of the 1,630 Bevin Boys up to the end of May 1944, ninety-four per cent were found to be satisfactory, whilst the remaining six per cent did not display interest in their work. Absenteeism was always a problem in the coalmining industry and during May 1944 proceedings were taken against four cases involving established miners and convictions obtained in three of them.

Northumberland and Durham suffered a series of strikes, in spite of a shortfall in output of coal of 30,000,000 tons. Yorkshire too had its share of disputes when, also in 1944, seventeen miners walked out of the pit after one of their colleagues had suffered an injury. Management agreed to drop proceedings provided the men agreed to the sum of £10 being deducted from their wages in respect of the broken bond. This was an agreement known as under bond not to strike during wartime. The men did not accept this, and were subsequently prosecuted and fined. In this region alone 80,000 summonses were issued in just two years. Lancashire and Cheshire also had its share of strikes, causing the loss of 150,000,000 tons of coal to the nation. On the other hand Nottinghamshire and Derbyshire seemed to have maintained a good output with few labour problems during 1944.

Despite the Union's objective for a 'closed shop', it should be said that the majority of Bevin Boys were not interested in joining a Trade Union, understandable as their feeling was that working in the coal mines was only temporary for the duration of the war, and they had no intention of making a career in the industry. Nevertheless, the trade unions felt that these young men should come under their wing and occasionally pressures of persuasion were used, as will be seen in the example letter given out to Bevin Boys working at the Bullcroft Main Colliery in South Yorkshire:

> Dear Friend.
> I think by now you should have almost become accustomed to your new sphere of working life (not a very kind way of getting a living, is it?)
> Anyhow I am instructed to inform you that everybody working underground at this pit are in the Union with the exception of a few of you new comers to the industry, and we think that you have now been here long enough to have joined the Y.M.A.
> So don't be different to all the rest of the pit. and please come and join at once, otherwise unfriendly decisions may be taken against you.

> *Signed on behalf of the committee.*

It was not until after the war, and the protracted release of the Bevin Boys from the industry, that some sort of backing and representation was sought. At Littleton and Hilton Main Collieries in South Staffordshire, Bevin Boys set up their own committee in August 1946, which resulted in a mass meeting held in Wolverhampton in March 1947 to consider grievances and injustices, with the question of release from the industry of paramount priority. This ultimately resulted in a two-day token strike by Bevin Boys in the Cannock area, in protest at the unfair demob rate, and to send a deputation to see M.P.s in London.

The general feeling was that of being tired of being kicked around and blamed for the inefficiency of the coal industry, as a local newspaper reported. Another newspaper said that the feeling of Bevin Boys was that they hated the sight of the pits, not because of the job, but because of the bullying by pit officials, who were supposed to be training and teaching them.

Although only about 350 Bevin Boys came out on the two-day token strike in November 1946. it was hoped that others throughout the country would follow suit. However, this token show of strength did not seem to gain the support that was needed, doubtless due to communication and co-ordination with other Bevin Boys in other regions being the problem and the fact that numbers were slowly diminishing by virtue of gradual demobilisation from the mines.

Fact and figures taken from PRO: CAB 102/399 H.M.S.O. 'Coal',
Colliery Guardian,

	1944	1945
Juveniles under eighteen	10,400	9,400
Ex-miners returned from H.M. Forces	6,400	11,500
Ex-miners recruited from other industries	6,900	8,100
Ballotees	15,000	5,900
Optants	8,500	7,200
Men, other than ex-miners, from H.M. Forces	4,700	2,000
Men, other than ex-miners, from other industries	4,900	3,700
Total	56,800	47,800

	Total number of trainees directed to pits			Number of Bevin Boys employed at coal face	Number of regular workers upgraded to coal face as result of 'Bevin Scheme'
Ballotees	Others	Total	coal face		
Northern 'A'					
Northumberland	1,165	674	1,839	130	719
Cumberland					
Northern 'B'					
Durham	4,115	2,663	6,778	611	2,303
North Western					
Lancashire					
Cheshire	1,302	2,560	3,862	290	1,501
North Wales					
North Eastern					
Yorkshire	5,027	4,959	9,986	460	2,387

North Midland					
Notts					
Derby	2,164	3,161	5,325	857	1,996
Leicestershire					
Midland					
Staffs					
Warwick	2,310	3,058	5,368	766	1,646
Cannock Chase, Shropshire					
Wales					
South Wales, Forest of Dean					
Bristol	2,586	2,315	4,901	2,895	not available
Somerset					
Scotland	1,305	1,768	3,073	398	456
South Eastern					
Kent	260	172	432	13	360
	20,234	21,330	41,564	6,420	11,368

Rectuitment and Wastage 1946/1947

	1946 (52 weeks)	1947 (53 weeks)
Recruitment		
Juveniles (under 18)	12,691	14,654
Ex-Miners from H.M. Forces	27,862	12,255
Ex-Miners from other industries	19,817	28,960
From Residential Training Centres	4,835	15,865
Others	7,615	22,456
Total	72,820	94,190
Wastage		
Net compensation and long-term sickness cases		
deaths and retirements	34,229	17,273
Released from the Industry by the	-	(19990
Ministry of Labour		
Released on Completion of National	42 789	(12 994
Service obligations		
Other Wastage	-	(17,768
Total	77,018	68,025
Net Intake or Outflow	-4,198	+26,165

Table of British coal output and productivity, 1938-1945

	1938	1939	1940	1941	1942	1943	1944	1945
No. of mines producing coal	1860	1856	1769	1737	1738	1690	1634	1570
Average no. of wage-earners on colliery books (000)	781.7	766.3	749.2	697.6	709.3	707.8	710.2	708.9
Saleable coal produced (mines) (m. tons)	227.0	231.3	224.3	206.3	203.6	194.5	184.1	174.7
Opencast coal production (m. tons)	-	-	-	-	1.3	4.4	8.6	8.1
Output per manshift (tons)								
at face	3.00	3.00	2.97	2.99	2.91	2.86*(2.75)	2.70	2.70
underground	1.49	1.49	1.45	1.44	1.40	1.38	1.34	1.33
overall	1.14	1.14	1.10	1.07	1.05	1.03	1.00	1.00
% of face shifts to total	38.03	37.85	37.04	35.96	35.94	35.94*(37.48)	37.19	36.96
Shifts possible	5.30	5.53	5.75	5.91	5.96	5.96†(5.85)	5.74	5.65
Shifts worked	4.96	5.15	5.27	5.37	5.34	5.24†(5.12)	4.96	4.73
% of absenteeism (all workers)	6.4	6.9	8.3	9.0	10.4	12.1†(12.4)	13.6	16.3

*O.M.S. statistics were based on a different definition of 'face workers' from 1943.
†New basis for statistics.

ANALYSIS OF NUMBER OF FACE-WORKERS IN DECEMBER, 1944 WITH COMPARATIVE FIGURES FOR

Districts	No. employed in coal cutting and cleaning out (machine cut faces)	Percentage of total face-workers	No. employed in filling (machine cut faces)	Percentage of total face-workers	No. of coal getters on hand-got faces	Percentage of total face-workers	Others employed at the face	Percentage of total face-workers	Total number of face-workers
		%		%		%		%	
Northumberland	1,817 (1,682)	12 (13)	6,116 (5,645)	42 (41)	508 (457)	3 (3)	6,278 (5,883)	43 (43)	14,719 (13,667)
Cumberland	164 (158)	8 (8)	948 (895)	48 (48)	266 (262)	14 (14)	600 (553)	30 (30)	1,980 (1,868)
Durham	2,246 (2,104)	5 (5)	5,800 (5,406)	14 (14)	15,875 (14,769)	37 (37)	19,159 (17,745)	44 (44)	43,080 (40,024)
South Yorkshire	2,239 (2,304)	6 (6)	12,081 (11,022)	32 (32)	8,263 (7,455)	22 (22)	15,126 (13,667)	40 (40)	37,709 (34,178)
West Yorkshire	1,450 (1,352)	8 (8)	5,377 (4,977)	31 (31)	5,174 (4,682)	29 (29)	5,706 (5,214)	32 (32)	17,707 (16,225)
North Derbyshire	1,161 (1,090)	8 (8)	6,032 (5,434)	40 (40)	373 (319)	2 (2)	7,70 (6,971)	50 (50)	15,266 (13,814)
Nottinghamshire	1,472 (1,343)	9 (9)	6,922 (6,095)	40 (40)	1,535 (1,360)	9 (9)	7,234 (6,473)	42 (42)	17,293 (15,271)
South Derbyshire	140 (121)	6 (5)	870 (813)	36 (37)	36 (33)	1 (2)	1,357 (1,241)	57 (56)	2,405 (2,208)
Leicestershire	246 (228)	8 (8)	1,218 (1,075)	41 (40)	67 (62)	2 (2)	1,453 (1,341)	49 (50)	2,984 (2,706)
Lancashire & Cheshire	1,319 (1,221)	7 (7)	6,000 (5,514)	32 (32)	1,781 (1,640)	9 (10)	9,725 (8,867)	52 (51)	18,825 (17,242)
North Wales	216 (212)	8 (8)	1,761 (1,165)	44 (44)	428 (401)	15 (15)	959 (854)	33 (33)	2,864 (2,632)
North Staffordshire	500 (460)	7 (7)	3,028 (2,730)	42 (41)	463 (426)	6 (6)	3,316 (3,030)	45 (46)	7,307 (6,646)
Cannock Chase	462 (428)	7 (8)	2,480 (2261)	40 (40)	924 (865)	14 (15)	2,417 (2,125)	39 (37)	6,283 (5,679)
South Staffordshire	16 (16)	1 (1)	119 (110)	9 (9)	947 (902)	71 (72)	246 (230)	19 (18)	1,328 (1,258)
Shropshire	64 (61)	8 (8)	220 (200)	27 (27)	164 (153)	20 (20)	366 (341)	45 (45)	814 (755)
Warwickshire	261 (244)	5 (5)	1,707 (1,590)	33 (34)	1,376 (1,264)	27 (27)	1,824 (1,627)	35 (34)	5,168 (4,725)
S. Wales & Monmouth	1,250 (1,170)	3 (3)	7,628 (7,049)	16 (16)	26,630 (24,375)	55 (55)	12,854 (1,848)	26 (26)	48,362 (44,442)
Forest of Dean	116 (110)	7 (7)	497 (445)	29 (28)	793 (646)	46 (40)	322 (397)	18 (25)	1,728 (1,598)
Bristol	2 (2)	2 (2)	4 (4)	3 (3)	118 (99)	95 (95)	– (–)	– (–)	124 (105)
Somerset	23 (23)	2 (2)	58 (55)	4 (4)	894 (838)	68 (69)	335 (305)	26 (25)	1,310 (1,221)
Fife	980 (947)	10 (10)	2,543 (2,490)	27 (27)	656 (645)	7 (7)	5,198 (5,071)	56 (56)	9,377 (9,153)
Lothians	571 (557)	14 (14)	1,064 (1,010)	26 (26)	809 (758)	20 (20)	1,639 (1,551)	40 (40)	4,083 (3,876)
Lanarkshire	2,082 (1,953)	12 (12)	5,598 (5,263)	32 (32)	1,570 (1,480)	9 (9)	8,165 (7,619)	47 (47)	17,415 (16,295)
Ayrshire	497 (486)	9 (10)	1,381 (1,320)	26 (26)	1,264 (1,184)	24 (23)	2,143 (2,965)	41 (41)	5,285 (5,055)
Kent	12 (12)	1 (1)	– (–)	– (–)	1,593 (1,422)	70 (71)	665 (565)	29 (28)	2,270 (1,999)
Great Britain	19,296 (18,014)	7 (7)	78,952 (72,568)	28 (28)	72,509 (66,477)	25 (25)	114 (105,583)	787 (40)	40 (262,642)

Note: Figures in brackets relate to effective employment, i.e. excluding wage-earners absent for the whole of the week for whatever cause.

Statistics Directorate,
Ministry of Fuel and Power,
7, Millbank, S. W. 1.
28th February, 1945.

Week ended 11th December, 1943

No. employed in coal cutting and cleaning out (machine cut faces)	Percentage of total face-workers	No. employed in filling (machine cut faces)	Percentage of total face-workers	No. of coal getters on hand-got faces	Percentage of total face-workers	Others employed at the face	Percentage of total face-workers	Total number of face-workers
	%		%		%		%	
1,820	12	6,170	42	524	3	6,310	43	14,824
(1,695)	12	(5,723)	42	(482)	3	(5,875)	43	(13,775)
172	9	930	45	371	18	580	28	2,053
(157)	8	(868)	45	(349)	18	(551)	29	(1,925)
2,127	5	5,642	14	15,893	39	17,208	42	40,870
(1,987)	5	(5,239)	14	(14,655)	39	(15,805)	42	(37,686)
2,105	6	11,398	30	9,602	25	14,692	39	37,797
(1,876)	6	(10,278)	30	(8,713)	26	(12,968)	38	(33,835)
1,421	8	5,226	30	5,580	31	5,506	31	17,733
(1,292)	8	(4,797)	30	(5,010)	31	(4,949)	31	(16,048)
1,150	8	5,738	38	684	5	7,384	49	14,956
(1,070)	8	(5,250)	39	(591)	4	(6,692)	49	(13,603)
1,495	9	7,055	40	1,797	10	7,102	41	17,449
(1,360)	9	(6,275)	40	(1,546)	10	(6,488)	41	(15,669)
149	6	859	36	8	–	1,397	58	2,413
(136)	6	(777)	36	(5)	–	(1,267)	58	(2,175)
244	9	1,130	41	103	4	1,267	45	2m744
(226)	9	(1,034)	42	(79)	3	(1,140)	45	(2,481)
1,350	7	6,205	33	1,800	9	9,698	51	19,053
(1,240)	7	(5,655)	33	(1,640)	9	(8,787)	51	(17,322)
200	7	1,238	45	511	18	824	30	2,773
(182)	8	(1,087)	45	(454)	19	(690)	28	(2,413)
516	7	3,043	41	532	7	3,347	45	7,438
(490)	8	(2,760)	41	(495)	7	(2,945)	44	(6,690)
450	7	2,297	37	1,150	19	2,284	37	6,181
(406)	7	(2,092)	38	(1,035)	19	(2,035)	36	(5,568)
14	1	121	9	936	72	226	18	1,297
(14)	1	(108)	9	(877)	74	(191)	16	(1,190)
46	6	196	27	184	26	296	41	722
(41)	7	(162)	26	(161)	26	(248)	41	(612)
263	5	1,677	32	1,419	27	1,906	36	5,265
(253)	5	(1,495)	32	(1,247)	27	(1,649)	36	(4,644)
1,193	3	7,845	16	27,435	57	11,710	24	48,184
(1,108)	3	(7,179)	16	(24,839)	57	(10,576)	24	(43,702)
106	7	467	29	821	50	241	14	1,635
(102)	7	(416)	28	(753)	51	(211)	14	(1,482)
6	5	7	5	116	90	–	–	129
(6)	5	(7)	6	(103)	89	(–)	–	(116)
20	1	61	4	944	69	346	26	1,371
(19)	1	(61)	5	(895)	72	(273)	22	(1,248)
952	10	2,432	26	635	7	5,318	57	9,337
(915)	10	(2,372)	26	(627)	7	(5,196)	57	(9,111)
541	13	1,149	28	934	22	1,545	37	4,169
(516)	13	(1,057)	27	(870)	23	(1,453)	37	(3,896)
2,190	12	5,903	33	1,550	9	8,303	46	17,945
(2,101)	12	(5,644)	33	(1,454)	9	(7,855)	46	(17,054)
480	9	1,347	25	1,311	25	2,170	41	5,308
(458)	9	(1,291)	25	(1,267)	25	(2,058)	41	(5,074)
–	–	–	–	1,512	72	583	28	2,095
(–)	–	(–)	–	(1,365)	72	(519)	28	(1,884)
19,010	7	78,137	27	76,352	27	110,243	39	283,742
(17,653)	7	(71,627)	27	(69,512)	27	(100,411)	39	(259,203)

COAL 11/101

10

Release and Recognition

The Government Debate in the House of Commons on 23 October 1945 certainly highlighted the question of release from the coalmining industry. Evidence of the fact of the protracted release of the Bevin Boy is clearly shown by the token strike carried out in November of the following year, although eventually the method of release brought in was that of the group number system, applied on the same lines as in the Forces.

The Joint National Negotiating Committee in May 1945 took up the matter of an issue of clothing that men received when released from the forces. This consisted of a battle dress, underclothes, two shirts, two pair of socks, one pair of boots or shoes, a civilian suit and a cap or hat. In addition there was a further issue of a civilian shirt, two more pairs of socks, a further pair of shoes and a civilian raincoat; the Bevin Boys never received any of these items.

The Committee then brought up matter of the non-issue of travel passes by the Government, and to allow additional days for travel before and after the Easter and Whitsun Holidays, when failure to do so would have a bad effect on the youngsters remaining in their hostels.

The unfortunate Bevin Boy certainly received a raw deal throughout, not only working in the pits but outside as well. Apart from the low pay, he had to endure whilst at work all the personal discomforts of heat, cold, draughts, damp and wet conditions, further aggravated by dirt and dust with the constant risks of accident and injury. Furthermore, there were no toilet facilities underground and some collieries were without pithead baths in which to wash at the end of a shift. Certainly the unsociable hours left much to be desired and would contribute to fatigue, and the granting of only one week's leave per annum, in addition to a day off on Christmas Day, gave little chance for recovery.

Off duty in the mining towns there was always a certain amount of resentment from the local mining families, who justifiably felt that the Bevin Boy should not be there at all and that their own kith and kin serving in the armed services should have remained in the pits. When travelling or in your home town, the fact of not being in the uniform of one of the services would attract attention, often resulting in abuse from members of the public, as well as challenges by local constables for the same reason. During wartime any such young person who looked of military age could be suspected as a call-up dodger or possible enemy spy. Bevin Boys had their

Ministry of Labour and National Services,
Local Office,
CANTERBURY.

RELEASE GROUP OF MAN SERVING IN MINING EMPLOYMENT AS AN ALTERNATIVE TO SERVICE IN H.M. FORCES

In reply to your enquiry as to your position under the above scheme you have been allocated Release Group Number .... 6 H .

* The date of release of this group has been reached and if you wish to obtain your release from the industry you should apply to the National Service Officer for permission to leave in the usual way, attaching this form to your application.

* The date of release of this group will be .... When that date is reached, if you wish to obtain your release from the industry apply to the National Service Officer for permission to leave, attaching this form to your application.

* The date of release of this group has not yet been announced and a further communication will be sent to you when that date is reached. In the meantime you should retain this form.

Mr. ....

.... National Service Officer

Date 27 FEB 1946

*Delete as appropriate.

E.D. 753 (Tear-off)

M00563   50M 1/46   CN&CoLtd 749 (6090)

civilian Identity Card endorsed by the Ministry of Labour and National Service.

Even the large service institutes, such as the NAAFI Clubs in towns and cities, were barred and of course the duty free concessionary rates for cigarettes and tobacco extended to service personnel did not apply.

The recognition part of this chapter is easily dealt with, for the answer is 'None'. Why then did the 48,000 or so Bevin Boys, whether ballotees, volunteers or optants, who served their King and Country by working in a coal mine in lieu of service in the forces, never receive any form of recognition? Apart from doubts that the scheme was a success in terms of the war effort - a possible source of embarrassment to the Government at that time - nevertheless these young men played their part in a vital role.

Today no records remain of these forgotten Bevin Boys as all Government records were destroyed during the nineteen fifties. Unless individuals kept personal documents, they cannot prove they ever served in the mines.

Many who served during the war in far less hazardous occupations received the award of the 'Defence Medal', but the Bevin Boy was not included. The Royal British Legion does not recognise the role of the Bevin Boy by allowing representation at the Festival of Remembrance.

One might ask, was it all worthwhile for the eighteen months from December 1943 to May 1945 when approximately 48,000 Bevin Boys were conscripted into the industry, 22,000 of them compulsorily. It was small wonder that a large number deserted during this time. As Mr. Arthur Horner, the Welsh Miners' Leader, said in Newport at the time, 'From our experience you cannot work the mines with forced labour.'

In keeping with the policy of Government Record Offices, pertaining to certain categories of records, a ten per cent sample is preserved for posterity, This is the case of Bevin Boy records covering the Midland region only and consists of returns from local Labour Exchange Offices listing names, registration number and training centre or colliery allocation for the period 1943-47.

11

Government Debate

House of Commons 23 October 1945 Directed Mineworkers

5.47 p.m.
Flight Lieutenant Teeling (Brighton):

I rise to bring before the House the question of the demobilisation of what are commonly called 'Bevin Boys'. In effect, that means conscripts for the mines, and also a considerable number of optants. I had hoped that the Minister of Labour would have been able to be present tonight, but I understand that he has gone abroad and I therefore hope that the Parliamentary Secretary, who is to reply, will put before him the points I wish to raise. I am not trying to raise them in any political sense but merely for this reason: That I understand, and have understood for some time, that the Ministry of Labour have in mind making a definite statement about the position of these boys. Nothing, however, has been done yet and these boys remain where they are, not knowing what is to happen to them. They are not only constituents of mine, but also constituents of almost every Member. There are well over 20,000 actual conscripts, and nearly 30,000 optants. making a total not far short of 50.000 young men from the ages of 18 up to 22. and up to about 30 in the case of optants.

These people, who have been brought from every part of the country, have no mining background. They come from every class of the community, and although they may be 100 per cent fit physically many of them are entirely unsuitable for life in the mines. It seems a great pity that the name of the former Minister of Labour should stick to these boys. I believe that unless we pay more attention to their position and unless we realise that the attempt to see whether we could do something to get more people into the mines has on the whole turned out to be a failure.

These young men will be wrecking their lives. There is a possibility in years to come that they will be the first to be on the dole and will also be physically wrecked, because of that experiment, which had not been a great success. They are mostly young boys who have no real chance of voicing their grievances, and who feel that they are very much the forgotten men in this country. So far as I can see from a quick look at HANSARD, and what I have heard myself, no reference whatever was made to these boys in yesterday's Demobilisation Debate. Yet in a sense they are mixed up with the Forces. When it was originally decided to try out this experiment the conscripts were boys who, normally, would have been called into the Services. They were not given the option of not being called into the Services. Large numbers were in different Air and Army Training Corps when they were forced against their will into this calling.

Certainly, the country was then given the impression that these boys were, in a sense, doing the same thing as fellows called in to the Forces. They complained that they would not have the glamour of being in the Services. Time and time again they were told, and were given the impression, that what they were doing was just as much a war-time job as any job in the Fighting Services. The optants were told when they left the Forces to go into the mines that it would count for their group towards release, Now I am told that that is not to be the case. Yet in the case of the Royal Air Force I gather that such service is to be counted. That is all wrong. Decisions must be made on this matter which will cover all the Services. So much for the optants. What about the conscripts? We have been told and it took some pressure to get the statement, that their service is now to be counted for group release as if they were in the Services. But which Service? Yesterday we heard about the Navy. Army and Air Force groups coming out at different times, and we were told that the reason was because of the size of the different groups. Here we have a new kind of Force. It is not sufficient answer to be told that they will come out in the same way as the Services, because they do not know which particular Service, Think of these young boys. They are the future men of this country, and we want to have good men in the years to come. They are thinking about their future.

Do not let us ever imagine that they intend to stay in the mines longer than necessary. I have been talking and travelling with them during the last month in Yorkshire, Northumberland, Cumberland and South Wales, and I can say without exaggeration that I did not meet more than one per cent who had any intention whatever of going on with mining. They said, 'What training are we going to have for our future'? Is experience as a haulier going to be of much use? Fellows in the Services may be trained as signallers or for any other of the innumerable jobs that have to be done there, but nothing is being done for us.' These boys have been sent to the mines, and then have been practically told to go to the devil. Are there any education officers? Are there any welfare officers? Only two or three, and. in some places none at all. Is anything being done in regard to vocational training.' No. Men in the three Services are to get gratuities. Are there to be gratuities for the Bevin Boys when they come out of the mine? I believe I am right in saying that we have passed an Act whereby people entering war service must be given their old jobs back when they have finished with that service. That does not apply in the mines. I know several boys who have been invalided out, and whose jobs have not been kept open for them because there has been no compulsion on their employers, because the boys are not entitled to get back into their pre-service jobs. Almost all the boys coming out of the mines beg to be allowed to return to their old jobs. They are most anxious to have some kind of training. It might be said that they have every opportunity in taking courses and reading. But the boys say, 'We are dog tired. We are not accustomed to this.' Boys of 15 to 19 are being made to do jobs in the mines which were previously done by miners of 24 or 25, who had been trained for some time. In South Wales, I found them being sent down some of our worst mines, mines which the average miner would not go down. It would have been much more to the point to send these boys down the best mines wherever possible, but they have been sent anywhere they have been needed. At one hostel, I met boys, this was in Doncaster, who had to walk one and a half miles to work to do a night shift from 9 p.m. to 6 a.m. They took with them sandwiches, which they had to pay for themselves, and had four pints of water during the night. Their own sweat and the coal just did not make those sandwiches particularly edible. Members might say that this is the ordinary life of the miner, so why-should these boys not have to do the same I do not say that they should not, but I say that if you are compelling young men to go into a job which miners go into voluntarily. (Hon. Members: 'No.') Well, at present not every miner is allowing his son to go into the mines. At one place, I saw 10 miners working; only two of their sons were going into the mines, whereas the eight others were Bevin Boys who had been forced into the mines. If you are going to force them into the mines then the same advantages and benefits as you are giving to the men you are sending into the Services.

What about their pay? These boys are not allowed lavish pay. They get about £3 10s. a week, whereas the waiters in this House get almost double that sum. The same applies to hostels, I saw and stayed in one where there should have been 400 boys, but where there were only 300. They were getting £3 10s. a week. Certain deductions amount to about 7s. 6d. and there is a further 30s, deducted for their hostel keep. That does not leave them with a very large income. In addition, these boys are given two leave passes a year, but they are only available between the months of April and September. I have seen some of these boys in Northumberland, who have come from my own area of Brighton. In two cases, boys wanted to go home to see their fathers on leave from the Front, in the months outside April and September, and they paid the full fares themselves. When some of us went into the Services, we were allowed Service rates. Why cannot these boys, if they are not allowed to go into the Services, many of them have been in the A.T.C. and other training corps, and are forced to go into mining, to be treated in the same way.

Absenteeism is a growing trouble. I would like the House to picture these boys as having just left school with their careers and lives in front of them. Normally, up to a point, they would be kept by their families or, if they were in the Services, everything would be done for them. They would be trained, educated and an eye would be kept on them: but these boys are in hostels and. although the staff do their level best, these boys are wasting their time completely when not down the mine. They have nothing to do. and no one tries to find anything for them to do. It is true that they play billiards and ping-pong, and get reasonably good food, but the point is that now they have been told they will not be prosecuted for not going down the mines, and so they are gradually drifting away. I met some of these boys, who told me, 'We only go down the mines now twice a week, because that pays for our hostel keep.' The rest of the time they waste hanging around doing nothing. Two other boys I met went down the mines very seldom, and when it came to a night-shift they did not go down at all. They were living in these hostels for young miners, and they went off digging potatoes for local farmers. Another boy went off as a taxi-driver. They are compelled by law to work in the mines, but when they get to the mines they are not compelled to go down them.

They are hanging about, and if you can imagine anything worse than that for boys of 18, 21, and 22. I, personally, cannot. I think that they sometimes think they are forgotten by the Government, and are not being bothered about because there are only 40,000 to 50.000 of them.

Something should be done to save these young men. They are not trained, and they are going to come on to the labour market in a hopeless condition, work-shy and completely ignorant of a trade, many of them, though not all. There are large numbers of them who are more than willing to work, but they are becoming less in number, because they get less encouragement from the Government and feel completely forgotten. I cannot get the figures from the Minister on absenteeism in the last two or three months, but I do not need to have them, because one can see it all the time. The rumour has gone round that they are not going to be prosecuted for not going down the mines, and the majority of them are slowly but surely giving up the idea of work in the mines. I do not know what the solution is. In peace time it is an appalling thing to think that any group of people in this country are being conscripted and forced into work which they do. What are the Government going to do about that?

These youths, in large numbers, have said to me, 'We would rather be in the Forces than here. It is wrecking our lives, and we hate it like poison.' They really do; you can see it in every hostel. Their argument, and I think it a reasonable one, is that under Class B there are numbers of miners serving in the Forces who have had two or three years training in the mines who would be far better able to do the job than they can. Why do you not force them to come back If you are going to have people under Class B who are vitally important to the country, it is no good saying in a lackadaisical way. 'You ought to come back.' If they are vitally needed, they should be made to come back. If you are going to need, as you do need, a large number of miners this winter, you will get far better work out of the men who know how to be miners if you get them back under Class B, and replace them by putting these boys in the Forces. These miners could be sent back, and the boys could be sent into the Services where they originally wanted to go.

Their present absenteeism does not mean that you announce in the morning that you are going to be absent next day or next week; it merely means that you do not like the weather and you go back to bed again, and do not tell anyone about it. The very fact that these boys do not turn up for work, is completely upsetting the shifts and organisation of the pits for many hours, and means loss of a considerable amount of time. That is going to increase unless something can be done. I think it is up to the Government to do something fairly soon about it. I would beg of the Government if they do not feel they can make a statement on this matter today to realise that there are these reasons, and that they are felt by thousands of boys all over the country. If these boys had been properly treated they might have become young ambassadors for the mining industry.

Mr. Hale (Oldham):

When the hon. and gallant Member talks about soldiers who have been miners, how long does he suggest that those who have served in Burma should be directed to the mines? Why is it that he says that 90 per cent of these lads who have been trained refuse to remain in the mines

Flight Lieutenant Teeling:

As to why 90 per cent of them do not want to stay in the mines, I have given some suggestions as to what I think are the reasons. As to the other point, I would only ask that these Class B men should remain compulsorily in the mines so long as the Bevin boys would be compelled to stay in the mines if they take their place.

6.10 p.m.
Mr. Blyton (Houghton-le-Spring)

I have listened with amazement to the statement made by the hon. and gallant Member opposite. I have just emerged out the pit after 32 years as a lodge secretary. We had a certain number of Bevin boys at a particular colliery, and I think it would be very unfair to suggest that these lads should have gratuities when they have been paid the trade union rates of wages for their work. It has been said that these lads have been forced into the pit. I myself was forced into the pit, not by direction of the Ministry of Labour, but by force of economic circumstances, I went into the pit to try to augment the family income in the early days of 1913, when the coal industry was a very thriving industry. Are these Bevin boys who now desire to get out because they do not like the conditions to have privilege over others who went into the mines? There are some good Bevin boys, and there are some that are round pegs in square holes. It is surprising to me to find the hon. and gallant Gentleman opposite arguing that absenteeism should increase, and making a statement which, in my opinion, might encourage that absenteeism.

When I heard the hon. and gallant Member talking about sandwiches and sweat, I recalled sweating without sandwiches. I remember that I coal-hewed five days a week, and took 35s, home for a wife and two children as a result of the policy that was pursued in the coal industry by hon. Members opposite when they were in Government, and dealing with the coal mining industry of this country. Mention has been made of water but the miner in the pit always had a glass of water by him, because water is the best thing to drink while in the pit. To talk about the miner drinking water is to try to convey something to this House which is a commonplace in the mining industry. I suggest that the fairest way of dealing with the Bevin Boys' problem is to apply the age plus service principle in the mines as in the Services. The hon. and gallant Gentleman suggested we should get these lads out of the pit. What is the use of the Minister of Fuel and Power urging an increase of output during the coming winter months, when the man-power in the pits had dropped from 713,000 in the last four months to 696.000. With lost man-power, we are asking the men to get more coal to tide us over this winter period, and then an hon. Member opposite suggests that we should worsen the position by releasing 40,000 to 50,000 haulage lads who are absolutely essential in the working of the coal mining industry. I suggest to the Minister of Fuel and Power that he will find that the men who have come out of the pit have done six years' service. The Essential Work Order in the mining industry was put into operation at the time of the capitulation of France in 1940. Men in the pit before that time were directed into the Army. These men have tasted a different life and have made up their minds, many of them, that they are not going back to the mining industry. Why should we force them back to release the Bevin Boys? As a miner, and a life long one, who has emerged out of the pit to become a Member of Parliament for a mining constituency. I say quite frankly that the eyes of this country will be opened to those who do not want their sons to go into the pit. I suggest the Minister of Fuel and Power should try to get our men to give us a greater output of coal, and not reduce the output by releasing Bevin boys on the lines suggested by the hon. and gallant Member, but release them on an age plus length of service basis as in the Forces. If he does that I am sure that in the period that lies ahead he will be able to give to the people in the blitzed houses the coal they need this winter.

6.15 p.m.
Lieutenant-Colonel Dower (Penrith and Cockermouth)

I think my hon. and gallant Friend the Member for Brighton (Flight-Lieutenant Teeling) has performed a public duty in bringing to light the conditions and problems connected with the Bevin boys. Those of us who were in the last Parliament, to whatever party we belonged, will agree that there have been many arguments on the question of these young men being drafted into the mines. I am not in the least saying whether it is more valuable service to be in the Army, or to be in that most honourable profession, a very distinguished profession, a very distinguished representative of which we have just heard, and whom we welcome in this House. He speaks with far more authority than I could ever do about the mines. These boys without exception were willing to fight, and if necessary die for their country.

Those of us who were serving in the House received a great many letters. Many of these lads had served in the cadet forces, had done pre-military training of some kind or another and were desirous of fighting for their country. Then down came the late Minister of Labour's order directing them into the mines, (An hon. Member: 'The Government's order'). That is so, I am not trying to make a party point, It was the Coalition Government's order. That created misery in the minds of these young lads. They went down the mines, and I think it is wrong to bring into this Debate a sugges-tion that anything wrong goes on in the mines. The mining industry must be made a magnificent industry. Why should it be considered a disgrace to go down the pit The point I am trying to make is that these lads want to fight for their country. If they had been balloted into any other industry, they would have felt just as disappointed as they did when they were directed into the mines. I would like to ask the Parliamentary Secretary to deal with this point when he comes to reply: I do not like the method of ballot by which some names come out, and because I do not like these lads having been prevented from fighting for their country, I ask him in all seriousness and in all sincerity, may we see fair play for these lads just as if they had fought for their country.

One point is that they are to have no medals. They will mix with their contempo-raries and will have nothing to show what they did in the war. Then again there is the economic point. I am solidly against direction of labour. My right hon. Friend knows that I fought the late Minister on that. I want to know whether these Bevin boys will have a period of leave following release, when they will be free to choose whatever work they would normally take, which is the privilege of the Serviceman when he is finally demobilised. Will they get their own jobs back? These are the main points. I am not trying to over stress the case. I am not trying to say that these boys have been treated most abominably. The whole country has had to go through a very difficult time, and every one of us has had to make sacrifices of a major nature. All I am interested in is to make absolutely sure that, wherever it is reasonable, these boys shall be treated as if they had served their country.

6.20 p.m.

Mr. Jack Jones (Bolton)

I speak in this debate not as a miner but I have had some little to do with the Bevin boys. For 10 months I was chairman of an Essential Works Order Tribunal where some of the Bevin boys who objected to being directed to the mines had to appear. If there is anything in this country at the moment to which it is desirable that patriotism should be applied it is the mining industry. I know of no reason why the sons of those who are not miners should not have their share of mining. I would that it had been possible to have Bevin Boys 30, 40 or 50 years ago. They would have brought back from the mine knowledge which would have been disseminated to their relatives and friends, which would have been of tremendous value to those who, because of economic circumstances, have to work in the mines. These boys are directed to the mines on a very fair ballot principle, but I know of no better people for the mines. They have had a good schooling, and statistics will prove that their average weight and physique is far better than the average of the miners' sons from the valleys and the mining areas. They are the people who should shoulder their own fair share of the things which were necessary to win the war, and, indeed, to win the peace.

I repeat that it would have been a good thing if we could have had some semblance of the Bevin boys 50 years ago. My advice to these youths would be that it is right in the interests of winning the war, and now primarily in the interests of winning the peace, that they should take their share of the things which some people have realised are very obnoxious things. It should not have been possible for a position to be reached in which people do not want to go back into the mining industry. Those people who allowed the industry so to degenerate that the mines are now in their present position are those who are now objecting to their sons doing something which they were quite willing that other people should do. Some of the young fellows whose lives have been spent in sheltered circumstances, and whose parents have to bear responsibility for the condition in which mining is today are objecting from doing their share to bring about the prosperity of this country.

I hope that the Government will refuse at this stage to release these boys. I have five children who have served in the war. They volunteered. They did not decide where they should go. If it was the submarine service, they went. If it was the Navy or Air Force they had to go, where they were directed. They had no option. They went in the interests of the country. They asked no credit for that, nor do I ask it for them; they are like millions of other people's sons. But there is every right, a moral and legal right, why these Bevin Boys who are objecting should be kept where they are if mining is of the importance which it is indicated as being. Without coal, whatever this Government or the people do. what is our position The Minister of Fuel and Power cannot get coal. Neither can the Cabinet nor the people who sit on these benches. It is only the men at the coal face who can get the coal, and these people should have to take their fair share in enabling the wealth of the country to be used throughout the whole social structure.

I say to the Government as one of its supporters that they should stick fast to the existing ruling, at all events until such time as the mining industry can be brought to a position where there will be no need for anyone to be balloted into the mine, no need for anyone to be forced into mining through their economic position. Let it be an honoured profession; mechanised, providing decent wages and conditions and then we shall have all we need of that most important commodity - coal. Without it we shall die.

6.25 p.m.
Mr. Orr-Ewing (Weston-super-Mare)

I do not think the House should be misled by the hon. Member who has just spoken and I do not think he meant his remarks to mislead the House. My hon. and gallant Friends and Members for Brighton (Flight Lieutenant Teeling) and Penrith and Cockermouth (Lieutenant-Colonel Dower) stressed that what they were out for was fair play. They were not arguing in support of the immediate release of Bevin boys, or in support of an agitation which claimed that these boys had been particularly unfairly used, Far from that, they made it quite clear that all they were out for was fair play on release and fair play throughout for these boys. That is a different matter. They pressed the Minister to make a statement to reassure their minds and the minds of the House and the country that fair play would be meted out to these boys. I do not think it would be quite fair to associate those who raised this matter with the words used by the hon. Member for Bolton (Mr. Jack Jones).

We are out for fair play. We are out to see that these boys are treated on the same terms as boys who have served in the Fighting Services. Nothing could do more harm to the mining industry than would be done if these boys were unfairly treated when they came out. The harm would be done to the industry far more than to the boys. I would like to stress that point more than anything else. I was born in a mining country, Ayrshire, and I have never lost my tremendous admiration for those who live in mining communities and work underground. We have to spread that knowledge. I do not believe that the experience of these boys will be lost on the country. If they come out feeling that they have been unfairly treated, they will not be too ready to help in the great work of spreading good news about the present and future of the coal mining industry, which is so vital not only to the welfare of those with whom they have been working, but to the country as a whole.

6.28 p.m.
The Parliamentary Secretary to the Ministry of Labour (Mr. Ness Edwards)

I listened with great interest to the statement of the case by the hon. and gallant Member for Brighton (Flight Lieutenant Teeling). When I saw his question I was impressed by the fairness of its wording and its obviously genuine desire to get information. I came along to the House this evening to give him and the House what I thought would be a reasoned reply. I am afraid that the way in which he has addressed the House has created the impression that Bevin boys, as a rule, are not playing their part in the national effort. I am afraid that in concentrating his criticism upon what is obviously a very small minority he has given the impression that the Bevin Boys are a liability to the mining industry. There was repeated later from the other side of the House the statement that the Bevin boys must have fair treatment. What is the assumption, that they are having unfair treatment? Is there that assumption fair (hon. Member: 'Yes'.)

The Bevin boys in the mining industry are getting parity of treatment with the rest of the boys in the industry. In the vast majority of cases they are getting preferential treatment. I was rather impressed with the last speaker's remarks about his concern for the men in the mining industry. I come to this problem not without some knowledge and I wish that concern had been shown many years ago, when as a boy of 13, I went down the pit to work for 9s. a week and had to walk four miles to my work and four miles home from work. It seems to me that this concern for the Bevin boys is a bit belated. The Bevin Boy is suffering as a consequence of the House of Commons not doing its duty to the mining industry years and years ago. I am sorry to introduce this feeling into the matter, but this Bevin Boy affair becomes a matter for politics in this country. We have to look at this very serious position in the mining industry, and we have to treat these boys fairly and with respect. There has been too much flippancy in this treatment of Bevin Boys in the mining industry. Let me deal with one or two points raised by the hon. and gallant Gentleman beyond the gangway. He raised the point about having no medals. Why should a miner have medals more than a gun-maker If we are to give medals, we must give them to the whole civilian population, and not least, to the housewives of Britain. I do not think that that is really a tenable proposition, and we cannot treat the Bevin Boys differently from the rest of the community.

Colonel Clarke (East Grinstead)

Surely, there is a difference. A great many miners volunteered and went into the Forces and got medals. These boys wanted to go into the Forces, but were not allowed to, and so did not have a chance to get a medal.

Mr. Ness Edwards

The hon. Gentleman forgets that there were thousands of boys in the mining industry who wanted to fight and get medals, and we would not let them go. I did not think that the talk about medals gets to the root of the problem at all, and if that were all there was in it I think the Bevin Boys would laugh. (Hon, Members: 'That is only a small point) I can only deal with one thing at a time, and I am trying to be quite fair to the hon. Gentlemen opposite who have raised these points; I would like to give them the answer as we see it.

Let me take the suggestion that the ballot was wrong. I think that the suggestion really ought not to be made from that side of the House. It was decided upon by the full House of Commons, by a Coalition Government. It was equitable and fair to everybody, and it means that boys who, by nature and upbringing, have to go and do a dirty job, a job that they do not like, are taken into a strange social community, and find the atmosphere completely alien to them. It is regrettable that any social atmosphere in Britain should be so distasteful to any section of the community as to produce this result. As a final indication of our desire to meet any justifiable complaints from Bevin Boys, the Minister of Fuel and Power yesterday met a deputation of them. He has given them certain undertakings and certain guarantees to investigate their legitimate complaints, to improve their hostels, to give them better facilities, to locate them in hostels nearer to pits and to try to improve their travelling time and welfare amenities. But here is the significant thing; the Government are doing more for the Bevin Boy than it does for the ordinary boy in the industry.

Mr. Orr-Ewing

May I interrupt? I do not mean to make a point out of it, but, surely, the words just used by the Parliamentary Secretary do record the fact that there were grievances of such nature that a deputation had to see the Minister of Fuel and Power. I am not rising to underline the fact that there was a deputation, but I do ask the Parliamentary Secretary to be fair. The difficulties were obviously of such a grave nature that the Minister himself had to receive a deputation.

Mr. Ness Edwards

What the Hon, Gentleman fails to realise is that, in ordinary circumstances, the Minister would only receive representatives from organised workers in the industry, and the Bevin Boys are part of that organisation, but in order that there should be no suspicion that there was any bias against them, the Minister received them, and discussed with them, what they regarded as grievances. The Minister went one step further. If there is any possibility of removing the things they complain of. even if it would mean improving their position with other men in the industry, the Minister is prepared to see what can be done.

Flight-Lieutenant Teeling

The hon. Gentleman has just said that, normally, the Minister would only meet representatives of the industry. Are these boys allowed, or entitled, to belong to a Miners' Union?

Mr. Ness Edwards

The hon. and gallant Gentleman in his speech said he had been speaking with these Bevin Boys. I am really astonished that he is asking a question about such an obvious, well known fact. The answer is that the Bevin Boys are not only encouraged, but that special steps are taken to link them up with the industry, and to present their grievances as accurately as possible.

Flight Lieutenant Teeling

Do they become members of a union'?

Mr. Ness Edwards

They do become members, one Bevin Boy is a member of the Yorkshire Miners' Union, and is in this House with the money subscribed by the Miners' Federation, so I think the complete answer is that Bevin Boys are encouraged to become members of the union, and to play a full part in the union. In one of the hostels, they have even representation on the Miners' lodge committee, so that, on that point, there can be no doubt at all. They are fully welcomed into the miners' organisation.

Now I come to one or two points raised in the opening stage of the Debate. To say. in this House, that Bevin boys' lives are being wrecked is. in my view, putting the matter far too high. Their lives are no more being wrecked than those of any other boys who were taken from their homes and sent into foreign parts, as were our Armed Forces. There is the same interruption of careers. That is all it is, and I should say that fighting in Burma might be adequately compared with the Bevin Boys' experiences in the pit. I do not think any impression ought to be created that because a Bevin Boy, or a young man, in this country goes into the mining industry to play his part in getting the coal, upon which the success of our war effort depended, he is wrecking his life.

Flight Lieutenant Teeling

I did not say that.

Mr. Ness Edwards

The hon. and gallant Gentleman says he did not say that, but I took it down. He said that all this scheme is doing is to wreck boys' lives.

Flight Lieutenant Teeling

I definitely gave the impression, I am sure, that their lives are being wrecked because there is so much absenteeism, and nothing is being done about it. They are left hanging around, and they have none of the educational facilities available to young men in the Services.

Mr. Ness Edwards

That was a bit of make weight thrown in. I am coming to these points; I have them here. We shall see how much substance there is in the allegation. In every Bevin boys' hostel in this country there is a welfare organisation; there is a welfare officer. The manager of the hostel is, in effect, the welfare officer for his hostel. That is mainly his job. Associated with each of these hostels is a miners' institute. In a case I know of in South Wales, all the facilities of the mining community are made available to these boys within a stone's throw of their hostel. To say that they are just allowed to run wild is, I think, not paying them a compliment. I have met many of them in the hostels and I have attended their debates and discussions, their meetings, their plays, and their dances, and I want to say that the standard of their conduct is as high as, if not higher than, that of any other section of the community in this country. Their behaviour, on the whole, is first class. There is nothing to complain about in their general behaviour.

The position, I am sorry to be speaking at such length, is that there are three categories. There are the Bevin Boys, so called the ballotees, there are the optants, and there are the volunteers, 50,000 men, altogether, in the mining industry. If the scheme is scrapped, and all these men are pulled out, what will be the effect upon the life of the community this winter? The next point the hon. and gallant Gentleman raised was that men in Class B should be brought out. So far, we have had 2,000 men out in Class B, but even if we had in Class B all the men we wanted, all the men planned to be got out, we should not be able to replace the Bevin Boys because of the normal wastage of manpower in the mining industry. We cannot afford to lose a single man in the industry in this winter. The position is really serious, and I would ask hon. Gentlemen on the other side of the House not to make the task this winter more difficult than it is, because so much depends upon it. The comfort of our people, the rehabilitation of our industry, the reconversion of our industry, the success of our economy, all depend on us getting an increase in the supply of coal. To let anyone go away at this stage would be to make the position worse than it is. There are one or two other small points. The first is with regard to the date of release.

Flight Lieutenant Teeling

The date of release is not a small point.

Mr. Ness Edwards

After yesterday's Debate one would have thought that the general impression was that there would be a general levelling up with regard to the date of release in each of the three Services. It is not challenged that the principle of release applying to the Armed Forces should apply to the Bevin Boys. That is regarded, I take it, as being equitable and fair. In order that it should be clear and easily understood, what is in mind is that the date of demobilisation of the Bevin Boys shall be the date on which they would have been demobilised had they been in the Army. That, I imagine, is not only fair, but is giving them almost favoured treatment.

Flight Lieutenant Teeling

That is what they want to know.

Mr. Ness Edwards

The next point is in regard to rights of reinstatement. Rights of reinstatement only apply to men in the Armed Forces, and to no one else. If it is to be given to the Bevin Boys, it must be given to the optants, to the volunteers, and to every man who has been directed to employment in this country during the war.

Flight Lieutenant Teeling

Surely it could be given to the optants who were in the Forces beforehand?

Mr. Ness Edwards

If they were in the Forces and came out under Class B. and they went back to their employment -

Flight Lieutenant Teeling

But -

Mr. Deputy Speaker

The hon. Member must allow the Minister to get on with his speech.

Mr. Ness Edwards

I am stating the fact. A man goes out in the class W.T.A. reserve, and goes as a nominated worker to his old employment, if his old employment is still available. He is, in fact, reinstated. If we are to have the Reinstatement Act applied to everybody, the House should have thought of that before.

Mr. Bowles (Nuneaton)

If my hon. Friend looks up the report of the Debate he will find that the Foreign Secretary, when he was Minister of Labour, said he was going to make special arrangements for these boys to be reinstated in civil employment.

Mr. Ness Edwards

I have no knowledge of that, and I have looked through the papers carefully. I recollect no assurance of that sort ever having been given by the right hon. Gentleman. Let us see to what the Bevin Boys are entitled. When they are demobilised they are entitled to training, to further education grants and to the benefits of the apprenticeship scheme. Those are the rights they have, rights that are not conferred on the ordinary industrial worker. Those rights are there, and those they will get. This matter is the subject of very close investigation, and, if I may say so, the Hon, gallant Gentleman's question has held up the decision. We were asked in the question by the hon. and gallant Gentleman not to take a decision until he had placed these considerations before the House. I do not know if he wants me to read the letter.

Flight Lieutenant Teeling

It was in a Question put last week.

Mr. Ness Edwards

Yes, and in a letter which followed it. As far as the Government are concerned, they want to give to the Bevin Boys every fair treatment that can be given to them. The vast majority of them have played a very great part in winning this war. A small minority of them have not been playing the game. I want to appeal to all the Bevin Boys, to the optants and to the volunteers, to see us through this winter and through all these difficulties, because upon their efforts will depend the success of our turnover from war to peace production.

Question put, and agreed to.
Adjourned accordingly at Twelve minutes to Seven o'clock.

Hansard

12

Postwar Changes

With the cessation of hostilities in 1945, the Bevin Boy could not expect to be immediately released from the industry, since plans for demobilisation were very much protracted, as it would take time to release ex-miners from the services in order to return to their own original jobs.

In fact, measures were taken to plug the gap by the Ministry of Fuel and Power and Colliery Managers by sending out letters to all Bevin Boys in an effort to persuade them to remain in the industry for the time being. Needless to say that response was inadequate and Polish and displaced persons were deployed into the mines as an interim measure to fill the manpower deficiency in the industry after the war. However, with the continuation of National Service, optants and volunteers still continued to serve in the coal mines.

On 1 January 1947 the coalmining industry became nationalised under the control of the National Coal Board. During this first year 41,000 ex-miners returned and about 53,000 other recruits who were entirely new to the industry had to be trained.

Prior to the vesting date, colliery companies had their own individual training schemes, whereas the Board took over and rearranged them into standard procedures, thus enabling entrants to groups of collieries to be trained together. By the end of the year 1979, preliminary training centres were in operation, of which none were residential. However, Adult Residential Training Centres were situated at Stoke-on-Trent, together with Bevin Boy Training Centres at Askern, Birley, Muircockhall and Oakdale which were still administered by the Ministry of Labour and National Service until the National Coal Board took over control of these centres on 1 October 1947. In addition two new juvenile residential training centres were established at Easington and New Kyo in Durham, which were under the control of the local education authority.

With the now established five-day working week, many new rules and regulations came into being, especially in all aspects of underground training, with special emphasis in the use of coal face machinery which was undertaken at the Mechanisation Training Centre in Sheffield, originally set up in 1943 by the joint Ministries of Fuel and Power and Labour and National Service.

The need to increase the number of underground workers was essential if coal production was to be increased in postwar Britain. The depletion of the work force caused by sickness, deaths, retirements and the release from the industry by the Ministry of Labour of men who had completed their national service obligations, which included the Bevin Boy into 1949, meant that substantial replacements would be needed.

A staff college at Nuneaton, established by the Ministry of Fuel and Power, was opened in 1946 in order to provide instruction for Training Officers who would be appointed under the new regulations. This led to new courses being introduced for Chief Practical Instructors and Head Colliery Lampmen and in April 1947, after the National Coal Board had taken over, courses were extended to Welfare Officers, Recruitment Officers and Training Centre Managers.

Today, with half a century now past, Bevin Boys, as with the miners and collieries in the United Kingdom, are rapidly becoming a distant memory, soon to be enveloped into the annals of history.

Those familiar pithead winding wheels over the shafts standing like sentinels on the skyline, together with the mountains of slag heaps, have almost vanished from the scene with only a handful remaining and with the passing of time yet another colliery closes down and the doors are shut on another chapter of coalmining history.

Inevitably the question remains as to why pit after pit had been closed down, causing unemployment and deserted towns, when coal is being imported from foreign countries. At the same time, modern technology in recent years, resulting in greater production requiring less manpower, and nuclear power as an alternative replacement would inevitably bring about a situation of the rapid decline of the coal industry in Britain.

Ministry of Fuel and Power,
7, Millbank.
London,
S.W.I
October, 1946.

Dear Friend,

If there is a shortage of coal this winter factories may have to close down and that would mean unemployment which we are anxious to avoid. I am doing everything possible to help the mineworkers. We have brought the mines under national ownership; the Government have agreed in principle to a five-day week which is now being discussed between the National Coal Board and the National Union of Mineworkers; and already we have made a start with payment for statutory holidays.

We want to give every mineworker security and prosperity and make up for the bad conditions of the past. I am doing all I can to get more workers into the industry, but this cannot be of much help this winter. We can only get the coal the country needs if you and your comrades get more coal per shift or if you work a fuller number of shifts every week. We could get all the coal we need if the men would attend regularly to their work and stop absenteeism. Please remember that when men absent themselves from work, whether at the coal face or on haulage work or in any other capacity, it brings about a reduction in coal output.

I appeal to you to give me your help to get the extra coal we need. By doing so you will give industry a chance, keep the home fires of the country supplied with fuel and give nationalisation a good start. I am trying to help you - please do what you can to help me.

Yours sincerely

E. Shinwell

Emanuel Shinwell became Minister of Fuel and Power from 1945.

The National Coal Board officially came into being on 1 January 1947.

The British Coal Industry became de-nationalised on 1 January 1995, reverting back to private ownership, exactly forty-eight years after it began.

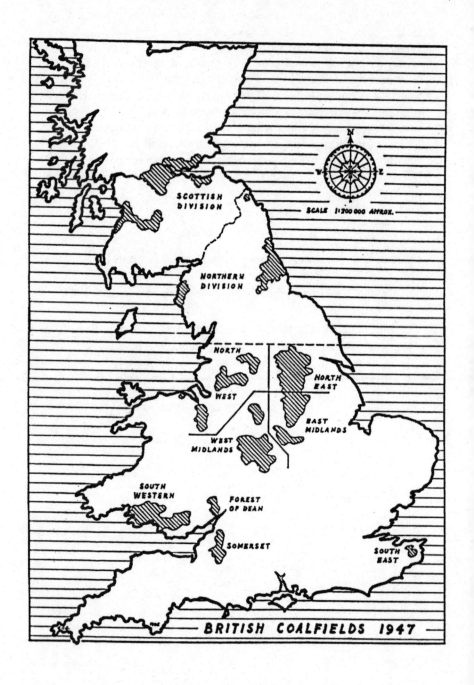

13

Statistics and List of Mines

The county statistical information for each division has been extracted from the Ministry of Fuel and Power list of Mines in Great Britain for 1945.

The figures given in respect of the persons employed (which include clerical and managerial staff) represent the number employed in December 1945, except in cases where mines had ceased working earlier in the year. In such cases the figures relate to the number of persons normally employed when the mine was at work.

Some mines produced substances in addition to coal, such as blaes (BL), fireclay (FC), ganister (GR), oil shale (OS), as well as ironstone. All are included in the totals of the figures presented, but fireclay or mainly fireclay and ironstone are also shown separately.

The lists of the mines include Pumping Pits or Stations and Ventilating Shafts, but exclude mines solely producing fireclay or ironstone.

No mines producing metalliferous products are included.

Training Centres for Bevin Boys are also shown in each division.

Location showing number of Collieries and Employees in each Division in 1945.

County	Collieries	Employees Below Ground	Employees Above Ground	Total
Scottish Division				
Ayr	56	8678	2742	11420
Clackmannan	9	819	214	1033
Dumbarton	9	1577	632	2209
Dumfries	3	996	307	1303
East Lothian	8	2192	711	2903
Fife	38	14219	4663	18882
(Muircockhall Training Centre)				
Lanark	148	18588	5336	23924
Midlothian	28	6897	2893	9790
Perth	1	15	5	20
Renfrew	1	5	-	5
Stirling	46	4033	1487	5520
Sutherland	1	11	5	16
West Lothian	36	5561	1906	7467
-	384	63591	20901	84492
Fireclay mines 40	Total employees 2535			

County	Collieries	Employees Below Ground	Employees Above Ground	Total
Northumberland and Cumberland Division				
Cumberland	19	4354	1490	5844
Northumberland	98	29479	10307	39786
(Cramlington Training Centre)				
-	117	33833	11797	45630
Fireclay mines 2	Total employees 6			
Durham Division				
Durham	218	80160	22717	102877
(Morrison Training Centre)				
(Horden Training Centre)				
York (North Riding)	9	1924	532	2456
-	227	82084	23249	105333
Ironstone mines 8	Total employees 2456			
Yorkshire Division				
York (South)	120	74989	19943	94932
(Askern Main Training Centre)				
(Birley East Pit Training Centre)				
York (West)	100	31257	9143	40400
(Prince of Wales Training Centre)				
-	220	106246	29086	135332
Fireclay mines 29	Total employees 247			
North Midland Division				
Derby (North)	85	29766	10395	40161
(Creswell Training Centre)				
Derby (South)	13	2674	1103	3777
Leicester	21	7789	2883	10672
Lincoln	2	98	49	147
Northampton	5	317	155	472
Nottingham	44	34439	11148	45587
-	170	75083	25733	100816
Fireclay mines 13	Total employees 111			
Ironstone mines 8	Total employees 619			
21	730			

County	Collieries	Employees Below Ground	Employees Above Ground	Total
North Western Division				
Cheshire	4	48	10	58
Lancashire	117	37380	13157	50537
(Newtown Training Centre)				
Denbigh	18	6368	2055	8423
Flint	2	388	173	561
-	141	44184	15395	59579
Fireclay mines 8	Total employees 43			
Cardiff Division				
Brecon (East)	2	55	14	69
Glamorgan (East)	108	31719	8024	39743
Gloucester (Bristol)	1	273	80	353
Gloucester (Forest of Dean)	45	3546	789	4335
Monmouth	87	26394	6009	32403
(Oakdale Training Centre)				
Somerset	12	2236	616	2852
-	255	64223	15532	79755
Fireclay mines 3	Total employees 74			
Swansea Division				
Brecon (West)	5	943	274	1217
Carmarthen	37	4753	1542	6295
Glamorgan (West)	123	23320	6386	29706
Pembroke	2	75	40	115
-	167	29091	8242	37333
Fireclay mines 4	Total employees 20			

County	Collieries	Employees Below Ground	Employees Above Ground	Total
Midland and Southern Division				
Kent	4	4771	1402	6173
(Chislet Training Centre)				
Salop	43	1652	618	2270
Stafford (North)	61	15357	5926	21283
(Kemball Training Centre)	36	13450	4801	18251
Stafford (South)				
Stafford (South) excluding	32	2819	966	3785
Cannock Chase				
Warwick	18	11241	3977	15218
(Haunchwood Training Centre)				
Worcester	11	426	153	579
-	205	49716	17843	67559

Fireclay mines 31.   Total employees 425.

County	Collieries	Employees Below Ground	Employees Above Ground	Total
Scottish	384	63591	20901	84492
Northumberland and	117	33833	11797	45630
Cumberland				
Durham	227	82084	23249	105333
Yorkshire	220	106246	29086	135332
North Midland	170	75083	25733	100816
North Western	141	44184	15395	59579
Cardiff	255	64223	15532	79755
Swansea	167	29091	8242	37333
Midland and Southern	205	49716	17843	67559
-	1886	548051	167778	715829

Fireclay mines	100	Total employees	3461	
Ironstone mines	16	Total employees	3074	
	16		6535	

List of Mines under the Coal Mines Act in Great Britain During 1945

Scotland Division

AYR

Afton No.1 (Abandoned 9/44)
Auchincruive Nos 1, 2, 3, 4, and 5
Ayr Nos. 1, 2, 9 and 10 Bank Nos. 1 and 6
Barony Nos. 1, 2 and 3
Benbain No.4 (Abandoned 11/45)
Beoch Nos. 2, 3 and 4
Bogton
Bowhill
Bridgend
Brockloch
Busbiehead No.3 (Mainly FC)
Chalmerston Nos. 4, 5, 6 and 7
Coalburn
Cronberry Moor
Fardalehill
Fortacre
Garrallan (A)
Greenhill
Highhouse Nos. 1 and 2
Houldsworth
Kames Nos. 1 and 2
Killochan
Knockshinnoch Castle
Little Mill Nos. 2 and 3
Lochwood No.2
Lugar
Mauchline Nos. 1, 2, 3 and 4
Maxwell
Montgomeryfield Nos. 1 and 2
Muirhouse
Muirside
Newfield
Newtonhead (Abandoned 9/45)
Pennyvenie Nos. 2, 3, 4 and 5
Polquhairn
Seaforth Nos. 1, 2 and 3
Shewalton Nos. 1, 2, 3, 4, 5, 6 and 7
Shieldmains Barbeth No.2 (Abandoned 12/44)
Shieldmains Drongan 6, 7 and 14

Shipmill Nos. 2 and 3 (Abandoned 11/45)
Southhook
Tofts Nos. 1 and 2
Warrix No.1
Whitehill Nos. 1 and 2

CLACKMANNAN

Brucefield
Craigrie
Devon
Devon No.3 (Meta Pit)
King O'Muirs
Melloch
Tillicoultry
Tulligarth
Zetland

DUMBARTON

Dullatur
Gartshore Nos. 1, 3, 9, 11 and 12
Gartshore No. 10, Twechar No.1
Saddler's Brae
Wester Gartshore

DUMFRIES

Fauldhead Nos. 1, 2, 3 and 4
Gateside Nos. 4 and 5
Tower Mine

EAST LOTHIAN

Bankton
Fleets
Glencairn
Limeylands
Penkaet
Preston Links
Prestongrange
Tynemount and Oxenford

FIFE

Aitken Nos. 1, 2 and Benarty

Balgonie
Benarty
Blairhall
Bowhill Nos. 1 and 2
Comrie
Cowdenbeath No.7
Cowdenbeath No. 10 (Kirkford)
Dean Nos. 3 and 4 (Abandoned 12/45)
Dundonald (Lady Helen and West Mine)
Dysart (Frances)
Elgin and Wellwood Leadside Pit No.2
Fordell
Glencraig
Isle of Canty
Jenny Gray
Kinglassie
Lassodie Estate No.2
Lindsay and Lindsay No.2
Little Raith (Gordon, Dora, Lochead Pits and
    Lochead Mine)
Lochgelly (Nelly and Mary)
Lochhead (Lochhead and Victoria Pits)
Lochore Nos. 1 and 2
Lochside Nos. 1, 2 and 3 (Mainly BL)
Lumphinans Nos. 1, 11 and 12
Michael
Minto
Mossbeath (Abandoned 3/45)
MUIRCOCKHALL (Training Centre)
Radernie
Randolph
Rosie
Thornton
Valleyfield
Wellesley
Wellsgreen
Windyedge

LANARK
Arbuckle No. 13 (Abandoned 3/45)
Ardenrigg No.6
Ashgill Mine
Ashlea No.3 (Abandoned 3/45) Ashlea No.4
    Auchengeich
Auchenheath (Mainly FC)

Auchlochan Nos. 2, 6, 7, 9 and 10
Auchmedan Mains
Aulton
Avonhead No.3
Bankend Nos. 8, 13, 15 and 16
Bardykes
Baton
Beaton's Lodge
Bedlay
Benhar
Bishop No.3
Blairmuckhill
Blantyre
Blantyreferme Nos. 1, 2 and 3
Boglea
Bothwell Castle Nos. 1, 2, 3 and 4
Braehead Farm
Braeside
Branchal
Broomknowe
Burnfoot
Burnside No.2 (Abandoned 12/45)
Calderhead Nos. 3 and 4
Canderrigg and Canderrigg Nos. 6 and 7
Carnbroe No.1
Cardowan Nos. 1 and 2
Castlehill No.6
Chapel
Chapelknowe (Abandoned 6/45)
Chapelrigg
Clachan No.1 (Abandoned 12/45)
Clachan No.2 (Abandoned 5/45)
Clarkston No.2
Coalhall Nos. 1 and 2
Coats-Park
Collyshot
Coursington
Crindledyke
Dalmacoulter (Abandoned 1/45)
Dalmacoulter No.2 (Abandoned 10/45)
Dalzell and Broomside
Dawn (Abandoned 6/45)
Dawn No. 2 (Abandoned 6/44)
Deerpark Douglas
Douglas Castle

Drumshangie No.4
Dryflat No.4
Dumobin
Duntilland
Fence
Femiegare
Forkens
Fortissat
Garscube
Gartness
Gateside
Gillhead
Glen
Glen (Nine Feet) (Abandoned 5/45)
Glentaggart
Glentore
Greenhead Nos. 1 and 2
Hamilton Palace
Hartrigg
Hassockrig
Headless Cross Nos 1 and 2
High Damgavil No.5
Hillhouserigg
Hills of Drumgray No.9 (Mainly BL)
Hills of Murdostown No.1
Hills of Murdostown No.2 (Abandoned 10/45)
Hopefield
Houldsworth (Abandoned 5/45)
Kennox Nos 6 and 7
Kepplehill and Stane Nos. 1, 2 and 3
Kingshill Nos. 1 and 2
Kippsbyre (Kiltongue)
Knowehead
Langside (Abandoned 3/45)
Langside No.2
Lochend No.5
Mauldslie
Netherton
Northfield and Hall
North Linrigg 5
North Shaws Overtown
Overwood
O'Wood
Palace Nos. 1 and 2
Parkneuk (Abandoned 5/45)

Quarter Nos. 1 and 2
Raebog No.6 (Abandoned 1945)
Rankin
Ross (Abandoned 7/45)
Royal George (Abandoned 10/45)
Shotlinn
Skellyton (Abandoned 6/45)
Skellyton Nos. 2 and 3
Southfield
South Langridge No.2
South Linridge No.6
Spalehall No.3 (Abandoned 3/45)
Spalehall Nos. 4 and 5
Spoutcroft No.2
Stanrigg No.4
Staylea
Swinstie
Tannochside (Abandoned 9/45)
Telfer (Abandoned 4/45)
Thankerton
Thinacres
Torrance
Townhead No.4
Wester Auchengeich
West Machan
Westoun
Whiteside
Wilsontown
Windsor No.2
Woodside

MIDLOTHIAN

Arniston
Baads No. 42
Burngrange Nos. 1 and 2 (OS)
Carberry and Wallyford Cornton
Dalkeith Nos. 1, 2, 3, 4, 5, 6, 8, 9, 10
Easthouses
Edgehead
Fraser (OS)
Gilmerton
Harwood
Lady Victoria
Lingerwood
Loanhead (Bur~hlee)

Loanhead (Ramsey)
Loganlea
Newbattle (Surface)
Newcraighall
Oxenford No.2
Polbeth No. 26 (OS)
Polton Roslin
Whitehill
Woodmuir
Woolmet

PERTH
Dollar

STIRLING
Auchengean
Balmore
Banknock No.3
Bannockburn
Birkhill No.3
Blackbraes Nos. 6 and 7
Blackston
Bonyside (Mainly FC)
Carronhall (Abandoned 11/45)
Drum (Mainly FC)
Drumbreck
Drumbroider (Abandoned 2/45)
Easter Jaw
East Plean Nos. 4 and 5
Ellrigg
Gateside Nos. 1 and 2
Greencraig
Herbertshire
Hill Farm
Holehousemuir
Jawcraig
Knowehead
Lime Road
Livingstone
Maddiston
Manor-Powis
Milnquarter (Mainly FC)
Okersdyke Nos. 2 and 3
Pirnhall
Policy

Polmaise Nos. 1, 2, 3 and 4
Redding No. 23 Stanley
Thatchrigg
Wester Burnhead No.2
Wester Shieldhill (Abandoned 1/43)

SUTHERLAND
Brora

WEST LOTHIAN
Armadale No. 15
Barbauchlaw
Blackrigg Nos. 1 and 3
Bridgeness No.6
Carriden
Drumback Nos. 1 and 2
Duddington Nos. 3 and 4 (OS)
Dumback Nos. 1 and 2
East Benhar No.2
Fauldhouse No.1
Foulshiels
Greenrigg
Heads
Hilderston
Hopetoun
Hopetoun No.5 (Glendevon) (OS)
Hopetoun Nos. 6 and 35 (OS)
Kinneil
Mid Breich (OS)
Muckraw
Murraysgate
Northrigg
Philpstoun Nos. 1 and 6 (OS)
Polkemmet
Riddochhill
Roman Camp Nos. 6 and 7 (OS)
Southrigg Nos. 3 and 4
Tottlywells No.1 (OS)
Westwood (OS)
Whitrigg
Whitrigg No.6 (Abandoned 5/44)
Woodend

Northumberland and Cumberland Division

CUMBERLAND

Allbright Drift and Birkby
Ayle, East Drift
Chapel Burn
Clarghyll Drift
Clifton
Ellenbank
Gillhead
Harrington No.5 (Mainly FC)
Harrington Nos. 10 and 11
Moorside Drift No.4
Moorhouse Guards (Abandoned 9/45)
Oakshawford Drift
Risehow
St Helens No.3
Solway
Walkmill
Whitehaven 'Haig', and 'Wellington' and 'William'

NORTHUMBERLAND

Acomb Drift
Arcot (Abandoned 12/45)
Ashington 'Bothal', 'Carl' and 'Duke'
Backworth 'Algernon', 'Prosperous', 'Bates', 'Fenwick', 'Eccles' and 'Maude'
Barmoor
Barrington and Bomarsund
Bates Pit
Bedlington 'A' and 'Doctor'
Blackhill
Bothal Drift Park
Broomhill
Burnhouse No.1
Burradon
Callerton
Cambois
Choppington 'A' and 'B'
Church Hill Drift No.1
Cowpen 'Isabella' and 'Mill'
CRAMLINGTON LAMB (Training Centre)
Crystal Well Drift

Dene House Drift (Abandoned 10/45)
Dinnington
Dudley
East Walbottle
Ellington
Elsdon
Eltringham Drift
Fell Drift
Fell End
Gapshields No.1 Gloria
Hareshaw Head
Harsondale (Mainly FC)
Hartford
Hauxley
Hazlerigg
Hedley Bank
Hedley Park
Henshaw Drift
Highfield Drift
Horton Grange
Lambley
Linton
Low Prudhoe Drift
Lynemouth
Mickley Bank
Mickley
Midgeholme East
Montagu Main
Moorwood
Nelson
Netherton 'Howard'
Newbiggin
New Delaval
New Hartley
North Drift
North Seaton
North Walbottle
Pegswood
Plashetts
Prestwick
Prior Drift
Ramshaw Drift
Rising Sun and Wallsend 'G' Robin Rock Drift
Scotswood Drift (Mainly FC)

Seaton Burn
Seaton Delaval
Seghill, 'Engine', 'John', 'Kitty' and 'Upcast'
Shilbottle 'Grange'
Slag Drift
Snope Burn Drift
Stagshaw Bank
Stobswood
Sutty Row
Throckley 'Blucher', 'Coronation', Isabella', 'Maria'
Tilesheds Drift
Townelev Drift
Weetslade
Wellsyke Drift (Abandoned 4/45)
West Clifton
West Sleekbum
West Wyham
Whinfield Drifts
Whinnetly Drift
Whittle
Whittonstall (Abandoned 6/40)
Williams Pit
Woodhom
Wood House Drift

Durham Division
DURHAM
Addison
Adventure
Allotment Drift
Alma
Auckland Park
Axwell Park
Aykley Heads
Beamish, 'James', 'Mary', 'Second'
Beamish Park
Bearpark, Brancepeth
Blackburn Fell Drift
Blackball
Blaydon Burn, 'Bessie' and 'Mary'
Boldon Nos. 1, 2 and 3
Bowburn including Tursdal
Brancepeth, A', 'B', 'C' Drift, 'Z'

Brandon
Brandon Pit House
Brusselton, Beaumont Drift
Brusselton, Busty Drift
Brusselton, Busty No.2 Drift
Brusselton, Harvey Drift
Brusselton, Hutton Drifts
Brusselton Tower
Bryans Leap (Abandoned 3/45)
Bryans Leap, Three Quarter Drift
Burnhope, 'Annie', 'Bettie' and 'Fortune'
Burnmoor 'D'
Burnopfield
Byer Moor
Castle Eden
Castle and Hutton Drifts
Chester South Moor
Chilton Nos. 1 and 2
Chopwell Nos. 1 and 3
Chopwell No.2 and Hutton Drift
Clara Vale
Cocken Drift
Cockfield Fell Drift
Copeland House
Cornsay
Craghead, 'Busty', Oswald' and 'Thomas'
Crookhall, 'Humber Hill', 'Victory' and 'Woodside Winnings'
Dawdon
Deaf Hill
Dean and Chapter Nos. 1, 2 and 3
Deanery
Dene Pit
Derwent
Duke of York Drift
Duke of York No.2
Dunston
Easington
East Hedley 'Hope', 'Post Office Drift' and 'Three Quarter Drift'
East Hetton
East Tanfield
Eden
Edge Drift
Eldon

Elemore
Emms Hill
Eppleton
Esh
Etherley Dene
Ewehurst
Ewehurst No.2
Fellwall
Fellwall Three Quarter Drift
Fellwall Five Quarter Drift
Finchale
Finlays Bank
Fishburn
Garesfield, 'Bute', 'Ruler', Tilley' Drift, Langley Park No.1, Langley Hall Drift
Garesfield, Langley Harvey Drift (Abandoned 10/42)
Garesfield, 'Lilley'
Grange
Greenhead No.2
Greenside and Stargate
Grewburn
Grewburn, 'Victoria' (Abandoned 4/45)
Hamsteels Clifford, Weatherhill and Ethel Drift
Hamsterley, Long Close Drift, Towneley Drift and Colt Park Drift
Handen Hold and Busty
Harraton
Harraton Annabella Drift (Abandoned 7/44)
Harton, Saint Hilda and Westoe
Hedley including 'Louisa New' and 'Morrison South'
Hedley Hill, Ballarat Drift and Three Quarter Drift
Hedley Hope (Abandoned 12/45)
Herrington
Hetton
Heworth
High Hazelwell
High Woodfield Busty (Abandoned 12/45)
Hill Top
Hill Top 'Harvey' and Low Main
Hindon Bridge
Hole-in-the-Wall

HORDEN (Training Centre)
Houghton including Hazard
Howle (Abandoned 9/45)
Hylton
Kelloe Winning
Kibblesworth, 'Glamis' and 'Robert'
Kimblesworth
Lady Durham
Ladysmith
Lanchester, 'Brockwell Drift', Harvey and Tilley Drifts
Lawsons Main
Leasingthorne
Leazes Drift
Littleburn
Louisa including MORRISON OLD (Training Centre)
Lumley, Sixth
Mainsforth including Bishop Middleham
Malton, Brockwell
Malton, North Amy Drift
Marley Hill
Marshall Green (Mainly FC)
Medomsley
Middlestone Moor
Morrison Busty
Mossy Burn
Mossy Burn, Top Main Drift
Mountset Fell Drift
Murton
Nettlebed No.3 (Abandoned 11/45)
Nettlesworth Drift and Waldridge Fell Drift
Newbottle, Dorothea
New Brancepeth
New Close Drift
Newfield Drift (Durham)
Newfield Drift (Peton Fell)
New Hargill Hill
Newton Cap
North Bitchburn
North Crane Row
North Tees
Old Eldon Drift
Old Etherley Nos 2 and 3
Ouston 'E' and Urpeth 'c'

Pan Lane, Three Quarter Drift
Pelton
Prince
Princes Street Nos. 1 and 2
Rackwood Drift
Ramshaw Nos. 1 and 2
Randolph and Gordon House
Ravensworth 'Ann', 'Betty', 'Shop' and 'Park Drift'
Roddymoor
Ryhope
Sacriston Five Quarter
Sacriston Shield Row
Seaham
Sherburn Hill
Shield Row Drift
Shotton
Silksworth
South Brancepeth
South Ewehurst Drift
South Garesfield
South Hetton
South Medomsley, 'Annie' and 'Drifts' Brass Thill Drift and Hutton Drifts
South Pelaw
South Shildon
Tanfeild Lea
Tanfield Moor, 'Willey'
Thornley
Thrislington
Towneley, 'Emma'
Trimdon Grange
Tudhoe
Tunnel Drift
Twizell Burn Drift
Ushaw Moor
Usworth
Vane-Tempest
Victoria Garesfield
Wardley
Washington 'F' and 'Glebe'
Watergate
Waterhouses
Wearmouth
West Auckland

West Morley
West Thornley, Main Coal Drift and Top Coal Drift
West Woodland
Wheatley Hill Nos. 1 and 2
Whitburn Nos. 1 and 2
Whitehouse
Whitworth Park
Wigglesworth No.2
Wingate Grange
Witton and Sascriston Busty
Woodside
Wooley

YORK (NORTH RIDING)
King's Pit (Abandoned 1945)

Yorkshire Division
YORK (South)
Aldwarke Main
ASKERN MAIN (Training Centre)
Bank Bottom Nos. 1, 3 and 4
Barnborough Main
Barnsley Main
Barrow
Beever Lane Bentley
Birley (Beighton Pit)
BIRLEY (East Pit) (Training Centre)
Bramley Hall No.2
Brierley
Broadhead
Broadhead Flatt and Low Matlock
Brodsworth Main
Bullcroft Main
Cadeby Main
Car House
Cliffe Bridge
Cottonwood
Darfield Main
Darton
Deame Valley
Denaby Main
Dinnington Main
Dodworth, Higham and Silkstone Fall
Dore (Mainly GR) (Abandoned 10/44)

Elsecar
Elsecar Main
Fell Lane
Fence
Ferry Moor
Frickley
Goldthorpe
Grange and Bradgate
Grimethorpe
Haigh
Haigh Moor (Abandoned 10/45)
Hatfield Main
Hemingfield
Hickleton Main
Highgate
High Hazels No.2
Houghton Main
Kilnhurst
Kiveton Park
Maltby Main
Manvers Main Nos. 1, 2 and 3
Margery Wood
Markham Main
Mitchell Main
Monckton Main Nos. 1, 2, 3, 4 and 5
Monk Bretton Moor
Moorend Silkstone
Mottram Wood (Abandoned 9/45)
New Silkstone
New Stubbin
North Gawber, Barnsley
North Gawber, Lidgett
Nunnery
Oaks Farm (Abandoned 8/45)
Orgreave
Parkwood (Mainly GR)
Primrose
Rob Royd and Strafford Silkstone
Rockingham
Rossington Main
Rotherham Main
Roundwood and Silverwood
Silkstone Common
Smithy Wood
South Rimsall

Stocksbridge
Strawberry Lea No.2 (Mainly GR)
Swallow Hill
Tankersley
Thimble Lodge (Abandoned 1/45)
Thimblewood
Thorncliffe
Thorne
Thurcroft Main
Townend (Abandoned 12/45)
Treeton
Usher Wood
Waleswood
Warren House
Wath Main
Wentworth Silkstone
Westfield
Wharncliffe Chase (Mainly GR)
Wharncliffe Silkstone
Wharncliffe
Woodmoor Nos. 1, 2, 3, 4 and 5
Wombwell Main
Woodend (Mainly GR)
Woolley, Barnsley
Woolley, Parkgate
Wortley No.2
Yorkshire Main

YORK (West)
Ackton Hall
Allerton Bywater
Allerton Main, Primrose Hill
Allerton Main, Victoria
Ambler Thorn (Mainly FC)
Ashday (Mainly FC)
Ash Grove No.1 (Mainly FC)
Bagden Wood
Barrowby
Bell String Nos 2 and 3 (Mainly FC) (Aban-
    doned 4/45)
Birkenshaw
Birks Fireclay (Mainly FC)
Boothstead
Bullcliffe Old Lane
Caphouse

Chatts Nos. 3 and 4
Cinder Hills and Quarry (Mainly FC)
Colls (Abandoned 4/45)
Combs
Crigglestone
East Ardsley
Ellen Royd and Horley Green (Mainly FC)
Emley No.3 Drift
Fallhouse Wood
Farnley including Ashfield and Whites (Mainly FC)
Fryston
Glass Houghton
Gomersal
Grange Ash
Greatfield
Gregory Spring
Hartley Bank
Hazlehead
Hemsworth
Horse Riggs No.2
Howroyd (New)
Ingham
Ledson Luck (Abandoned 11/45)
Lepton Edge and Whitley Clough
Lofthouse
Manor
Middleton, Broom
Middleton, New
Newmarket Silkstone
Newmillerdam
New Mytholme (Mainly FC)
Norwood Green
Nostell
Old Roundwood
Park Hill Park Mill
Peckfield
Prince of Wales (Midgley)
PRINCE OF WALES (pontefract) (Training Centre)
Roadside Nos. 1 and 2 (Mainly FC)
Robin Hood (Jane)
Rothwell, Haigh, Beeston, Fanny and Rose
School Wells Drift
Sharlston

Sharlston West
Shaw Cross
Shibden Hall
Shuttle Eye
Sledbrook
Snydale
South Kirkby
Springfield Farm (Mainly FC)
St John's Stone
Stoney Royd
Street Lane (Mainly FC)
Sunny Vale (Mainly FC)
Swindell Hill (Abandoned 2/45)
Toftshaw Moor
Tong Lane (Mainly FC)
Upton
Victoria No.1 (Mainly FC)
Victoria No.2
Walterclough (Mainly FC)
Water Haigh
Waterloo Main (Park)
Waterloo Main (Temple)
West Riding
Wheldale
Whitwood
Woolley Edge

North Midland Division
DERBY NORTH
Alfreton
Arkwright
Barlborough Common No.1
Barlborough Common No.2 (Abandoned 4/45)
Beighton Fields
Blackwell' A' and 'B' Winning
Bolsover
Bond's Main
Bramley Hall (Abaondoned 6/44)
Brimington
Britain
Brookhill and Plymouth No.2
Butterley Drift
Campbell, Hartington, Ireland and Calow Drift
Clay Cross (Park House) Nos. 2 and 7

Cobnar Wood
Coppice No.1
Coppice No.3 and Mickley
Cotes Park Nos. 2 and 3
CRESWELL (Training Centre)
Denby
Denby Hall Nos. 1 and 2
Dent Main
Diglee Drift
Doe Lea
Firth Wood
Furnace Hill No.3
Furness Clough (Mainly FC)
Glapwell Nos. 1 and 3
Grassmoor Nos. 1, 4 and 12
Handley Nos. 1 and 2
Hartshay
Hirst Hollow
Holbrook No.2 (Norwood)
Holbrook No.3 and Westhorpe
Hollis Nos. 1 and 2
Holmewood Nos. 2 and 3
Hunloke
Langwith
Larkhill (Abandoned 1/45)
Lindway Lane (Mainly GR)
Manners
Mapperley Nos 1 and 2
Markham No.1 Blackdale, No.2 Ell and No.4
    Deep Hard
Moor Side
Morton Nos. 5 and 6
Newbold (Mainly FC)
New Langley
New Marsh Lane
Oakerthorpe Drift
Ormonde
Oxcroft Nos. 1, 3 and 5
Pilsley Nos. 2 and 3
Pleasley
Quarry
Ramcroft
Renishaw Park
Ripley
Scarsdale

Shirebrook
Shirland
South Normanton
Stanley and Hillside
Swanwick (New)
Swanwick (Old)
Upper Hartshay
Wheeldon Mill Nos 1 and 2
Whitecotes Nos. 1, 2 and 3
Whitwell
Williamthorpe
Wingfield Manor
Wingfield Park
Wingfield Park No.2 (Mainly FC)
Woodside Nos. 1, 2 and 3

DERBY SOUTH
Bretby
Cadley Hill Nos 1, 2 and 3
Cadley, Little Coal
Church Gresley Nos. 1 and 2
Granville Nos. 1 and 2
Netherseal
New England (Mainly Clay)
Swadlincote Nos. 1, 2 and 3 T
horntree Drift
Thorntree No.2

LEICESTER
Bagworth Deep
Bagworth Main
Calcutta
Desford Nos. 1 and 2
Donisthorpe Nos. 1 and 2
Ellistown No.1
Fishley (Abandoned 2/45)
Holwell
Measham Main Nos. 1, 2 and 3
Merrylees
Nailstone Nos. 1 and 2
New Lount
Oakthorpe
Rawdon
Reservior
Snibston

South Leicestershire Nos. 1 and 2
Whitwick

NOTTINGHAM
Annesley
Babbington (Cinderhill No.1)
Bentinck
Bestwood including Calverton
Bilsthorpe
Blidworth
Brinsley and Selston
Bulwell (Abandoned 9/45)
Cinderhill No.4
Clifton
Clipstone Cossall
Firbeck Main
Gedling Nos 1 and 2
Grange Nos. 1 and 2
Harper Hill
Harworth
High Park
Hucknall Nos. 1 and 2
Kirkby including Lowmoor
Langton Nos. 7 and 8
Linby
Lodge Nos. 1 and 2
Mansfield
Manton Nos. 1, 2 and 3
Moor Green
New Hucknall Nos. 1, 2 and 3
New Selston
Newstead
Ollerton
Pye Hill
Radford and Wollaton Rufford
Sherwood
Shireoaks Nos. 1, 2 and 3
Silver Hill Nos. 1 and 2
Steetley Sutton
Teversal
Thoresby
Trowell Moor
Warsop Main
Watnall Welheck

North Western Division
CHESHIRE
Bakestonedale (Mainly FC)
Dales Green No.2
Ludworth Moor
Mount View (Abandoned 7/45)

LANCASHIRE
Albert
Alexandra
Altham 'Moorfields'
Arch Lane
Arch Lane Nos. 2, 3 and 4
Ashton
Ashton Moss
Ashton's Field
Brackley and Wharton Hall
Astley Green Avenue
Bamford Closes Bank Hall Baxter
Bedford Nos. 1 and 3
Beechwood
Bickershaw Nos. 1, 2, 3, 4 and 5
Billinge Lane
Blackclough, Lower Mountain Bold
Bradford
Brynn Hall Nos. 2 and 3 (Abandoned 11/45)
Calder, Huncoat and Scaitcliffe
Carr and Craggs
Chanters Nos. 1 and 2
Chisnall Hall Nos. 1 and 2
Cleworth Hall Nos. 1, 2 and 3
Clifton
Clock Face
Clough Head, Inchfield Moor
Copy
Cronton
Crow Knowl
Dalton Lees
Deerplay
Duxbury
Dyneley
Ellerbeck
Ellesmere
Farnworth Bridge
Garswood Hall Nos. 2, 3, 5, 6 and 7

Gauntly No.1 (Mainly FC)
Giants Hall
Gibfield
Gin and St George's
Golborne
Grime Bridge
Grime Bridge No.2
Hapton Valley
Hartshead (Mainly FC)
Harts Lane (Abandoned 8/45)
Higher Brooks, Middle Place Drift
Hoddlesden No. 12
Holland Moor
Holland Moor No.2
Howe Bridge
John and Taylor Pits
Ladyshore, 'Owl Hole' and 'Victoria'
Landgate
Lea Green, 'King', 'Queen' Nos. 1 and 2
Long Lane
Lyme (and Railway and Works)
Mains
Martholme
Maypole
Montcliffe
Moor Lane Drift
Mosley Common Nos. 1, 2, 3, 4 and 5
Moss Nos 3, 4, 5 and 6
Moston
Mountains
Nabb
Newton
NEWTOWN (Training Centre)
Nook
Oak, Victoria
Old Boston
Old Meadows
Parsonage Pemberton
Ravenhead Nos. 10 and 11 and St Helens'
    Alexandra'
Red Earth Drift (Mainly FC)
Reegley
Rough Bank
Sandhole
Sandy Road

Scout Moor
Stacksteads
Stacksteads, Top Pit (Abandoned 4/45)
Summersales
Sutton Manor
Tarbuck Farm
Tarbuck Farm No.2
The Park
Todmorden Moor Nos. 1 and 2
Towneley Demesne, Boggart and Park Vic-
    toria (Rumworth)
Victoria (Standish) Wain
Waterside (Belthom) (Mainly FC)
Welch
Whittle and Day Eye
Wheatsheaf
Wigan Junction Nos 3 and 4
Wildersmoor (Mainly FC)
Windy Arbour
Woodpark

DENBIGH
Bersham
Black Lane
Black Park
Brynkinalt including Ifton shaft
Coedpoeth (Abandoned 6/45)
Delph (Mainly FC)
Glascoed Adit (Abandoned 1944)
Glascoed (Mainly FC)
Gresford
Hafod Nos. 1 and 2
Llay Hall
Llay Main
Rhos Adit (Mainly FC)
Smelt (Mainly FC)
Smelt No.2
Woodlands

FLINT
Park Hill No.2
Point of Ayr

Cardiff Division
BRECON (EAST)
Llamarch (Slant) and New Clydach
Waen-Pwll-Dwr, Level

GLAMORGAN (EAST)
Aberaman and Abercumboi
Aberaman Clay (Level) (Abandoned 3/38)
Abergorki
Albion
Anthony and Pandy
Bedlinog
Bedlinog Cross, Measures Drift and
    Nantyffin Drift
Bertie and Trefor
Blaenclydach Drift
Bodringallt (Abandoned 1936)
Bute, Gorllwyn Level and Lady Margaret
    (Abandoned 1945)
Bute Level
Bwllfa Dare Nos. 1 and 3 (abandoned 5/36)
Bwllfa Dare No.2
Bwllfa New Drift No.4
Cambrian Navigation Nos. 1, 2 and 4
Cambrian Navigation No.3 (Abandoned
    1936)
Castle
Cethin
Cilely
Coedly Nos. 1 and 2
Cuckoo Level (Abandoned during war)
Cwmaman, Fforchwen and Trewen (Aban-
    doned 1935)
Cwm Cynon
Cwmglo Drift
Cwm Margaret, Mildred and Maritime
Cwmneol
Dare
Deep Duffryn and Navigation Deep Navi-
    gation
Dowlais Cardiff
Eastern
Ely
Ferndale Nos. 1. 5 and 9
Femdale No.6 (Abandoned 7/35)

Femdale No.8 (Abandoned 12/34)
Femhill Nos. 1, 2, 3 and 4
Fforchaman No.7 (Abandoned 4/35)
Ffynona Duon Level
Gelli, Steam
Gilfach (Shaft)
Glenrhondda Nos. 1 and 2 Shafts
Glenrhondda No.2 Level
Graig Nos. 1 and 2
Groesfaen
Hafod No.1
Lady Lewis
Lady Windsor
Llanbradach Nos. 1, 2 and 3
Llanharan, North and South
Llantrisant, North and South and House Coal
    (Abandoned 5/41)
Llwynhelig (Slant) (Abandoned 1934)
Llwynpia Nos. 1 and 2 (Abandoned 8/45)
Llwynpia Nos. 4 and 6
Lower Duffryn (Abandoned 9/27)
Lucy Thomas Nos. 1, 4 and 5
Maindy
Maindy (Level)
Mardy Nos. 1 and 2 (Abandoned 7/32)
Mardy Nos. 3 and 4
Merthyr Dare (Level) (Abandoned 6/31)
Merthyr Vale Nos. 1 and 2
Nantrodyn (Abandoned 8/37)
Nantyfedw (Level)
National Nos. 1 and 2 and Ynishir Nos. 1 and
    2
Nebo (Level)
New Drifts Nos. 1 and 2 (Abandoned 12/32)
New Gellingaer (Level)
New Rockwood
New Rockwood No.2
Ogilvie
Park No.1 and 2 and Sinking Pit
Penallta Nos. 1 and 2 Pit
Penrikyber Nos. 1, 2 and 3 Pits
Pentwyn Level
Penydarran (Level)
Penywaun (Level)
Pidwellt (Level)

Pontgarrig Drift
Pwllgwaun
Rhigos
Rhymney Merthyr No.2 (Abandoned 1940)
River Level
South Duffryn Nos. 1 and 2 (Abandoned 1940)
Southend
Taff Merthyr
Taff Rhondda
Tir Herbert (Slant) and Coronation Level
Tower Slant and No.3 Drift
Trelewis Level
Tydraw
Tyladu Level
Tymawr
Werfa Dare (Level)
Werntarw (Drift), Hafod Seam and Werntarw Pit
Windsor
Ynysfaio Nos. 3 and 4

GLOUCESTER (BRISTOL)
Coalpit Heath

GLOUCESTER (FOREST OF DEAN)
Addis Hill
Arles Level
Arles Level No.2
Arthur and Edward
Barnhill (Abandoned 6/45)
Berry Hill
Bixslade
Cannop Nos. 1 and 2 and Drift
Dark Hill Level
Drybrook Folly No.3
Eastern United Farmers Folly
Garbrook No.4
Heywood No.2 (Abandoned 8/44)
High Meadow
Hillersland No.2
Hollybush Farm
Jones Yorkley No.2
Mapleford Engine No.3
Mapleford Nos. 4, 5 and 6

New Fancy and Parkend Royal (Abandoned 1/45)
New Found Out Level
New Speedwell
Nine Wells
Norchard
Northern United
Old Drum
Princess Royal
Redding Horne
Speculation No.2 Drift
Speedwell No.2 (Abandoned 9/41)
Thatch (Abandoned 1940)
True Blue and Newnham Bottom
Union
Vallets Gale
Winnel No.3
Winnell Colliery Gale
Worcester No.3
Worrall Hill No.2 (Abandoned 3/44)
Wynol's Hill Nos. 2 and 3
Wynols Trenchard

MONMOUTH
Aberbeeg South
Abercarn (Prince of Wales and Quarry Pits) (Abandoned 1936)
Albion Road
Arrail Griffin Nos. 4 and 5
Bargoed, Brithdir, North and South
Bedwas Navigation
Beynon, including Lower Deep and North Blaina
Big Pit
Balck Vein (Level)
Blaencuffin
Blaendare
Bleanduar No.2
Blaenserchan and Llanerch
Britannia
Bush, New Level
Cern Coch Level
Cern Crib (Abandoned 7/42)
Cern Islwyn Drift (Abandoned 8/40)
Celynen North and Graig Fawr

Celynen South Nos. 1 and 3
Cwm Carn Nos. 1 and 2
Cwmtillery Red Ash
Darren Level
Deakin's and No. 10 Slopes (Slants)
Elled (Level and Mynydd Maen (Slant)
Elliot East and West Erskine
Garn Slope
Glyn Pit
Glyn Tillery (Level)
Golynos Slant (Mainly FC)
Graigddu Fireclay (Level) (Mainly FC)
Gray (Abandoned 10/27), Tillery (Abandoned 1938) and Vivian
Gwaelodywaun
Gwenallt
Hafodarthen
Hafodyrynys
Hill Drift
Islwyn (Level)
Kay's Slope
Llanhilleth Red Ash and Steam Coal
Llanover
Major Red Ash
Manmoel
Marine Nos. 1 and 2
Markham
McLaren Merthyr Nos. 1 and 3
Milfraen Pit
Millbrook South (Level) Navigation (Crumlin)
Navigation (Sirhowy)
New Tredegar
Nine Mile Point, East and West Pit
OAKDALE Navigation Steam and Waterloo Pit (Training Centre)
Old Black Vein,
Risca Nos. 1 and 2
Old Duffrys Drift
Pengam
Pentrepiod (Abandoned 8/44)
Pentwyn (Level)
Penyrheol
Plantation Level (Abandoned 3/44)
Plantation Level No.2

Pochin Nos. 1 and 2
Powell's Navigation
Primrose Levels
Prince of Wales (Abandoned 6/30)
Red Ash Level
Rhiw
Rhiw Colbren (Level Nos. 2 and 5)
Rock
Rock Vein Pit
South Wales Cwmtillery Nos. 1 and 2 and Rose Heyworth
Tir Pentwys
Travellers Rest (Level)
Tunnel Level
Ty Trist Nos. 1 and 2
Varteg Hill Top Pits, Mine Slope, New Slope and Rock (Pit and Slants) (Abandoned 7/32)
Verdun No.2
Viaduct (Level) (Mainly FC)
Watercourses
Waun Llwyd Nos. 1 and 2
West Blaina Red Ash (Level)
Wyllie

SOMERSET
Braysdown
Bromley
Camerton
Charmborough
Kilmersdon
Marsh Lane
New Rock
Norton Hill
Old Mills: Old Mills and Springfield Pits
Pensford
Radstock
Writhlington, Huish and Foxcote
Swansea Division

BRECON (WEST)
Abercrave and International (Slant)
Brynhenllys (Slant)
Diamond (Slant)

Waunlwydd (Slant) (Abandoned 3/45)
Yniscedwyn (Slant)

CARMARTHEN
Ammanford No.2 (Slant)
Blaenhirwaun (Pit)
Carway (Slant)
Castle (Level)
Cwm Capel
Emlyn Nos. 1 and 2
Erw
Gallyceidrim Nos. 1 and 2 (Slant)
Glanamman (Slant)
Goodig Level (Abandoned 3/45)
Great Mountain Nos. 1 and 2 (Slant)
Gwndwngwyn Jubilee (Slant)
Llandebie (Slant)
Llwynadda (Slant)
Llwyn-yr-haf Morlais (Pit)
Mount
New Cross Hands (Slant)
New Dynant (Slant)
New Lodge (Mainly FC)
Pant (Slant)
Pantyffynnon (Slant)
Pentremawr (Slant)
Pentremawr No.4 (Slant)
Pontyberem Glynhebog (Slant) and Great
    Mountain No.3
Pwll No.1 (Level) (Mainly FC)
Rhengog Fawr (Level) (Abandoned 5/45)
Saron (Slant)
Stradey (Level) (Mainly FC)
Talyclyn (Slant)
Top (Slant)
Wernos (Slant)
Ysguborfawr Nos. 2 and 3 (Abandoned 12/
    45)

GLAMORGAN (WEST)
Aberbaiden (Slant)
Abergelli (Slant) and Clydach Merthyr (Slant)
Avon (Pit)
Avon Hill (Level)
Blaenant (Level)
Blue Anchor

Braichycymmer (Pit) and Ffaldau (Pit)
    (Abandoned 11/45)
Bridge (Level)
Britannic (Pit) and Trane (Pit)
Broadoak (Pit)
Brynlliw (Pit)
Bryn Navigation (Slant)
Brynteg Nos. 1 and 2 (Slant)
Bryn Varteg (Slant) (Abandoned 8/45)
Bwllfa Ddu (Level)
Cae Duke
Caerau (Pit)
Castell (Slant)
Cern Coed (Pit)
Cern Drim (Slant)
Coedcae (Level)
Coegnant, North and South Pits
Coronation (Level)
Cwm No.2 (Level)
Cwm Evan Bach No.2
Cwmgorse (Slant)
Cwmgwrach (Drifts)
Cwmllynfell (Pit)
Cynon (Level)
Daren (Level)
Darran (Level)
D Day (opened 7/44, Abandoned 10/45)
Dillwyn (Slant)
Dillwyn No.2
Duffryn Rhondda (Slant)
Duffryn Rhondda Nos. 1 and 2 (Pits)
Eryl No.2
Farmers Level
Felinfran and Guerets (Slant)
Fernland No.1
Fernland No.2
Ffaldydre (Level)
Garngoch Nos. 1 and 3 Pits
Garth (Levels) Garth Merthyr
Garw (Pit)
Gleison (Pit) Glen
Glenavon Levels
Glengarw (Pit and Slant)
Glenhafod (Level)
Glyncastle (Pit)

Glyncoch (Level)
Glyncorrwg (Pit)
Glynogwr (Slant)
Graigavon (Level)
Graig Merthyr (Slant)
Gwaun-cae-Gurwen, East Pit, Maerdy Pit and Steer Pit
Hendy Merthyr (Slant), Tylwdyn and Maesmelyn
Hillside (Level) Hillside No.2
International (Pit)
Llwyndu (Level)
Maesmelyn (Level)
Maesteg Deep (Slant)
Marine (Level)
Mountain (Level)
Mountain (Pit)
Mynydd Newydd (Slant)
Nantewlaeth (Drift)
Nantewlaeth (Pit)
New Gellihir
New Gelli Hir No.2 (Level)
Newlands (Slant)
New Mountain (Level)
New Yniscu (Level)
North Rhondda No.1 and 2 Drift
Onllwyn Four Feet and No.1 Drift
Onllwyn Trigloyn (Slant) and No.3 (Slant)
Park Level Peacock
Penlan No.1 (Abandoned 9/45)
Penllwyngwent (Slant)
Penquar
Penrhys
Penrhys No.2 (Abandoned 12/45)
Pentre (Slant)
Pentwyn No.2
Priors Meadow (Abandoned 12/45)
Priors Meadow Gleilyd (Slant) (Abandoned 12/45)
Pwllbach (Slant)
Pwllfaron (Drifts)
Rhas
Rhigos No.1 (Level)
Rhigos Nos. 4 and 6
Rock (Slant)

Rock No.2 (Level)
Seven Sisters (Pit)
Skewen Main No.4 (Level)
St John's North and South Pits
Ton Phillip (Level) (Abandoned 1/45)
Torymynydd (Slant)
Tygwyn (Abandoned 3/45)
Tynygraig
Tyn-y-waun
Tytalwyn
Tytalwyn No.3
Varteg
Waun
Wernfawr West (Drift)
West End No.2
Western (Pit)
Wyndham Nos. 1 and 2 Pits
Ynisarwed (Drift)
Ystalyfera

PEMBROKE
Hook, New Drift
Wood Level

Midland & Southern Division
KENT
Betteshanger
CHISLET (Training Centre)
Snowdown
Tilmanstone

SALOP
Alveley and Highley Nos. 1 and 2
Benthall Coal Pit (Abandoned 10/43)
Benthall (Mainly FC)
Brandlee No.2
Common Nos. 1, 2 and 3
Deerleap (abandoned 10/40)
Farm (abandoned 1/44)
Farm No.2
Good Hope (Mainly FC)
Grange
Granville
Huntington

Kemberton including Halesfield
Lawley Coppice Nos. 1, 2, 3, 4, 7, 8, 9, 10, 11
    and 12
Lawley Coppice Nos. 5 and 6 (Abandoned
    11/41)
Lawley Drift Extension
New Works No.3 (Shortwood)
New Works No.4
Old Park
Plants Farm
Princes End
Randle Rock
Shortwood Nos. 5 and 6
Shrubbery
Smalley Hill No.1 (Mainly FC)
Smalley Hill No.2
Station Nos 1 and 2
Swan
Wellington No.5
Woodside

STAFFORD (NORTH)
Alsagers Bank
Apedale Hall Footrail (Abandoned 8/45)
Apedale Hall Footrail Nos. 2 and 3
Berry Hill including New Top (Deep) and
    Knowles
Burley Lane
Cannel Row (Abandoned 1/45)
Clough Hall No.3 (Abandoned 3/45)
Florence Nos. 1 and 2
Folly
Foxfield including Park Hall
Gillow Heath
Glass House No.1
Glass House No.2 (Abandoned 6/41) Glebe
Hall Field No.1 (Abandoned 11/44)
Hall Field No.2
Hayes Wood No.8 (Abandoned 3/45)
Hayes Wood No.9
Heathcote Road Footrail No.3
Holditch
Hollinwood
Leycett
Merryhill No.1 (Abandoned 1/44)

Merryhill Nos. 4 and 5
Miry Wood No.2
Mitchells Wood
Mossfield
Mount No.4
New Apedale Footrail
New High Carr Footrail
North Midland Norton
Park Hall Nos. 5 and 6
Parkhouse
Parklands Nos. 1 and 3
Parklands No.2
Podmore Hall Footrail
Ravenscliffe No.3
Redhall
Red Street
Red Street No.2
Rookery
Shelton Deep
Silverdale
Sneyd Nos. 1, 2 and 4
Stafford No.1 including KEMBALL (Train-
    ing Centre), Pender, Bourne and Hem
    Heath
Stafford No.2 including Sutherland and
    Homer
Talke Green No.5
The Beeches
Victoria
Watermills Footrail No.4 (Abandoned 3/45)
Watermills Footrail Nos. 5 and 6
Whitfield Hesketh, Middle and Winstanley,
    Institute and Platt
Wolstanton
Wood House Footrail No.1 (Abandoned 7/
    45)
Wood House Footrail No.3
Woodstock Footrail No.3

STAFFORD (SOUTH)
(CANNOCK CHASE)
Ashcroft (Abandoned)
Brereton including Brick Kiln Nos. 1 and 2,
    Old Engine Shaft, and New
Day Drift

Brownhills including Grove Bulls Meadow No.2

Caddick's Farm

Cannock Chase including Nos. 3, 7, 8 and 9

Cannock and Leacroft

Cannock Old Coppice

Cannock Wood

Conduit Nos. 3 and 4

Coppice

Coppice Farm

Coppice Farm No.2

East Cannock

Hilton Main Nos. 1 and 2

Holly Bank Nos. 3, 5, 7 and 15

Kingswood

Littleton Nos. 2 and 3 Pits

Mid Cannock

Nook and Wyrley

Old Wilkin No.8

Pool Hayes (Neachells Lane)

Pool Lane

Sling (Abandoned 8/45)

Spring Meadow (Abandoned 3/41)

Spring Meadow No.2

Walsall Wood

West Cannock No.1, 2 and 3 Mine, No.5 Mine (Downcast) and No.5 Mine (Upcast)

West Coppice

Wilkin

Wimblebury

Wyrley No.3

Yard Drift No.2

STAFFORD (SOUTH) (EXCLUDING CANNOCK CHASE)

Alley (Abandoned 12/43)

Amblecote No.2 (Mainly FC)

Baggeridge

Castle Farm No.1 (Mainly FC)

Cottage Pit No.2

Delph No.7 (Tintam Abbey)

Dibdale Nos. 1 and 2 (Mainly FC)

Dibdale No.3

Dock Drift No.2 (Abandoned 11/45)

Ellowes

Ettingshall Hall Farm (Mainly FC) (Abandoned 9/44)

Furnace

Grosvenor No.1 (Mainly FC)

Hamstead

Hawbush No.2 (Mainly FC)

Lodge

Milking Bank (Mainly FC)

Mount Pleasant No.2

Old Park No. 30 (Abandoned 1944)

Old Park (New Drift) (Abandoned 11/45)

Sandwell Park 'Jubilee'

Standhills C

Upper Gornal No.1 (Mainly FC)

WARWICK

Alvecote

Ansley Hall

Arley

Armington

Baddesley

Binley

Birch Coppice Nos. 1, 2 and 3

Coventry Nos. 1 and 2

Exhall (Abandoned 5/43)

Griff Clara Nos 1 and 2

Griff No.4

HAUNCHWOOD (Training Centre)

Hawkesbury

Kingsbury and Dexter

Newdigate

Pooley Hall

Tunnel

WORCESTER

Bay ton No.6 and Drift' A'

Beech Tree

Coombs Wood

Hurst (Clay) No.5

New Drift

Old Yew Tree Hill (Mainly FC) (Abandoned 3/45)

Simms Lane No.2 Smiths No.1

Thornleieh No.2 (Mainly FC)

Change of Divisions

Pre-1947 *(Private Ownership)*	Post-1947 *(National Coal Board)*
Scottish	Scottish
Northumberland	Northern
Cumberland Durham Yorkshire	North Eastern
North Midland	East Midland
North Western	North Western
Midland and Southern	West Midlands
Cardiff Swansea	South Western
Cardiff	Forest of Dean
Cardiff	Somerset and Bristol
Midland and Southern	South East

14

Addendum

A Bevin Boy Association was re-formed in recent years and is currently managed by a committee from around Stoke-on-Trent in Staffordshire, the area being influenced by the number of collieries that once thrived in that region, Chatterley Whitfield was one such colliery, at one time being the largest pit in the country and the first in Britain to produce one million tons output of coal per year.

Chatterley Whitfield became a Mining Museum in 1979 and had been the location for four consecutive annual Bevin Boy reunions. Sadly the Museum went into receivership in 1993 and the fifth annual reunion, which was also the fiftieth anniversary, was held at the Florence Colliery Social Club near Stoke-on-Trent. The occasion was celebrated by over 300 members amidst the filming by A.D. Films of a documentary production for Central Television, the title being 'The Bevin Boys'.

Fortunately three collieries have been preserved as Mining Museums: Caphouse Colliery near Wakefield, Yorkshire, England; The Big Pit at Blaenafon, Gwent, South Wales: Lady Victoria Colliery, Newtongrange, near Edinburgh, Scotland: Eden Camp at Malton in North Yorkshire depicts the story of civilian life during World War II and has an exhibit on the role of the Bevin Boy.

On the occasion of the 50th Anniversary of VE Day in London, the Bevin Boys were officially recognised in speeches made by Her Majesty Queen Elizabeth II, The Rt. Hon. John Major M.P., Prime Minister, and The Rt. Hon. Betty Boothroyd M.P., Speaker of the House of Commons.

Additional Mining Museums are located at:
Beamish - North of England Open Air Museum, County Durham.
The Black County Museum - Dudley, West Midlands.
Cannock Chase Valley Heritage Centre - Hednesford.
Cefn Coed Colliery Museum - near Neath, South Wales.
Radstock Mining Museum.
Rhondda Heritage Park (Lewis Merthyr Colliery) Mining Museum - Trehafod.
Woodhorn Mining Museum - Ashington, Northumberland.

A group of Bevin Boys outside Ystrad Mynach Miners' Hostel.
(Reproduced by permission of T. G. Fairbrother.)

Chatterley Whitfield Colliery.
(Photo: author.)

Caphouse Colliery (Yorkshire Mining Museum).
(Photo: author.)

Big Pit Colliery (Mining Museum).
(Photo: author.)

Lady Victoria Colliery. - Scottish Mining Museum.
(Photo: author.)

The Author at the 'Big Pit'. 1994.
(Photo: author.)

Group of Bevin Boys at Cramlington, October 1944.
(Photo: by courtesy of S. Bocknell.)

Typical Nissen huts built to accommodate Bevin Boys on Hostel sites.
The photograph is of Pelaw Bank Miners' Hostel at Chester-le-Street.
(Photo: P. Grisby.)

Bevin Boys 50th Anniversary re-union in November 1993 at the Florence Colliery Social Club, Stoke on Trent. In the background can be seen the colliery, demolished a year later. The author is standing in the front row. (Photo: author.)

Annfield Plain in 1994, previous site of several collieries which included Morrison Old Pit, one of the Training Centres. The preserved building on the left once formed part of the Morrison 'Busty' Colliery. (Photo: author)

Site of Horden Colliery in 1994. This colliery closed in 1986.
(Photo: author)

Site of Oakdale Colliery, 1994.
(Photo: author.)

Glossary of Mining Terms

Backs	Interior workings of mine
Bank	Area surrounding pit head
Banksman	Person in charge of cage on the surface
Bars	Flat planks of wood
Blocks/Dump!ings	Wooden wedges
Brattice	A partition to control ventilation
Cage	Shaft lift
Chock	Roof support
Clamping	Method of fastening from tub to overhead cable with use of clamp
Collier	Miner working at the coal face
Cog	Empty area left after removal of coal
Corporal	Another name for Deputy
Deputy	Person responsible for fire safety
Dinting	Lowering of tunnel floor
Downcast	Downward flow of air
Drag	Metal bar anchored to rear tub to prevent roiling backwards
Drams	Welsh term for tubs
Drift	A sloping tunnel extending from the surface down to underground workings
Face	Coalface
Fault	Layer of rock between coal
Gaffer	Foreman
Haulage	Transport of coal
Hewer	Miner who cuts coal
Hutches	Scottish term for tubs
Inbye	Empty tubs travelling into mine
Jack catches	Automatic safety catch to prevent tubs running backwards
Jazz Rails	Curved track on gradient
Journey	Number of tubs
Juts	Stop bars
Knocker	Person signalling to stop start engine
Lashing	Attaching rope to front and rear of tubs
Limbers	Horse/pony limbers
Linesman	Person painting line in centre of tunnel roof
Lockers	Metal or wooden bar for placing in spokes of tub wheels to prevent rolling
Long Wall	British term for coal face

Main and Tail	Front and rear attachment of rope to tubs
Mandrel	Miner's pick
Moggies	Mice
Mottie	Numbered disc - lamp check
Nick in	Cutting coal at face bottom
Onsetter	Person in charge of cage underground
Ostler	Person responsible for care of horses and ponies
Outbye	Full tubs travelling to pit bottom
Overman	Miner in charge of a district
Packing	Roof support
Paddy	Term for riding on tubs
Pit	Name for colliery or coal mine or area around the shaft
Puddy	Water Bottle
Puffer	Person responsible for payment to contract workers
Ripping	Raising and supporting of tunnel roof
Roadman	Track maintenance worker
Roadway	Underground tunnel
Refuge	Safety crevice in side of tunnel walls
Runner	Breakaway tubs
Seam	Layer of coal
Set of gears	Two vertical posts with horizontal lintel
Shaft	Vertical tunnel for cage
Shot firer	Miner responsible for boring holes and placing of charges
Slough	Metal rope strands becoming tangled during movement
Snap	Term for eating break
Squezees	Tub arresters at loading positions
Snap tin	Miners container for food
Stable	Shaft between seams
Stable	Area in which ponies and horses are housed
Stall	Compartment in which coal is worked
Stint	Area of coal face worked in a shift
Tally	Disc or token
Tram	Another term for tub
Trees	Pit props
Trunk road	Main roadway of mine
Tubs	Four-wheeled narrow gauge truck for conveying coal
Undercut	Area cut at bottom of coalface for hand extraction of coal
Upcast	Upward flow of air

Today's Colliery Sites

A visit to the original training centre colliery sites during 1994 had revealed the following changes:

Cramlington Lamb Little remains other than a few derelict buildings used by small contractors. A number of rows of miners' cottages still remain in occupation.

Old Morrison and Morrison Busty is now a busy industrial complex developed by the Durham County Council, consisting of a waste disposal depot, garden centre and a number of small firms.

Horden has only a pumping station remaining and this was being broken up at the time of my visit. Two halves of a winding wheel mark the site of the colliery, with one or two old buildings still standing.

Askern Main contains a few derelict buildings, the site now being used as a coke dump. Two halves of a winding wheel mark the site of the colliery.

Birley East had a few derelict buildings with only one being occupied by a small firm. The rest of the area is now common land for walking and horse riding. Two concrete stone blocks mark the position of the two shafts.

Prince of Wales is now a drift mine, the original shafts having been removed in 1981. Closed in 2002.

Newtown had completely gone, the area being now a housing estate and open park land.

Creswell has a large number of derelict buildings remaining, of which two are classified as listed buildings, one being occupied by the D.H.S.S. Some buildings at the colliery site and the old Bevin Boy prefabricated building hostel close by are used by small motor traders.

Haunchwood is now a modern industrial and housing estate. There are warnings and signs of mining subsidence in the area.

Oakdale has been completely razed to the ground with only the N.C.B. sign remaining at the entrance. The area is now used by walkers and, although flat, blends in with the small surrounding old slag heaps delicately camouflaged by nature. Three gas escape vents have been sunk into the ground. Now a housing Estate.

Muircockhall has a few derelict buildings once used by the Y.T.S. and a private company. The area is overgrown and now blends with the surrounding countryside.

Kemball is nor a derelict site with the Training Centre closed down. A new by-pass road is currently under construction.

Chislet has an industrial trading estate which includes a council waste disposal plant, surrounded by derelict waste ground.

Bibliography

Government Publications and Records

Public Records Office
CAB 71/10   Railways (Coal stocks).
CAB 71/12   Estimates of Voluntary Transfers.
CAB 102/399   The Bevin Boy Scheme.
COAL 11/101   Absenteeism in the Coal Mining Industry.
LAB 6/226   Direction of Men aged 18 25 into Coal Mining.
LAB 6/227   Men Selected for Coal Mining and Manner in Dealing with
                 Plea for Deferment or Postponement of Transfer on Hardship
                 Grounds.
LAB 8/406   Manpower Problems in Coal Mining 1941.
LAB 8/407   Recruitment of Juveniles to the Coal Mining Industry 1941.
LAB 8/409   Question of Increased Production and Supply of Labour in the
                 Coal Mining Industry 1941.
LAB 8/410   Increase of Production and Supply of Labour in the Coal Min-
                 ing Industry.
LAB 8/411   Increase of Production and Supply of Labour in the Coal Min-
                 ing Industry.
LAB 8/412   Increase of Production and Supply of Labour in the Coal Min-
                 ing Industry,
LAB 8/413   Minutes of a Meeting between the Minister and Secretary of
                 Mines about Manpower for the Coal Mining Industry 1941.
LAB 8/462   Memorandum setting out Problems of Future Manpower for
                 the Coal Mining Industry 1941-1942.
LAB 8/513   Question of Increased Production and Supply of Labour in the
                 Coal Mining Industry 1941-1943.
LAB 8/734   Direction of National Service Registrants to Coal Mining 1943.
LAB 8/763   Measures for Increasing the Number of Workers in the Coal
                 Mining Industry.
LAB 8/765   Allocation to the Coal Mining Industry of Men Registered
                 under the National Service Acts.
LAB 8/908   Direction of National Service Registrants to Coal Mining.
LAB 8/1157   Coal Mining Industry.
LAB 8/1241   Essential Work (Coal Mining Industry) Order,
LAB 8/1473   Coal Mining Industry - History of Labour Supply since May
                 1940.
LAB 18/107   Training for the Coal Mining Industry - Rules and Condition
                 for Trainees.

LAB 18/121	Coal Mining Training Scheme Sheffield (Mechanised) Premises.
LAB 18/209	Coal Mining Training (Post War Training Arrangements).
LAB 22/188	Panic Bevin Boy Hostel Programme.
LAB 37/16	Mobilisation of Labour for Industry - Coal Mining.
LAB 45/94	Coal Mining Ballot - HQ General Correspondence.
LAB 45/95	Coal Mining - Optants. Ballotees and Volunteers Allocated to Training.
LAB 45/96	Coal Mining - Allocation of Ballotees - Midlands.
LAB 45/97	Ballotees released from Coal Mining.
LAB 45/98	Recalcitrant Miners.
LAB 45/99	Mining Optants - Midland Region.
LAB 45/100	Record of Men Recommended for Release from the Coal Mining Industry - Midland Region.
POWE 16/88	Regional Controllers Conference held on 22 November 1944.
WORKS 22/186	Plans of Miners' Hostels.
WORKS 22/188	Miners' Hostels.

British Library

H.M.S.O. Publications

BS 69/6	Investigation into Serious Coal Mining Accidents (Nos. 10/21/22/23/24/25).

'Coal'

Bevin Boy by Derek Agnew (Published by George Allen and Unwin)
The Bevin Boy by David Day (Published by Ashford, Buchan and Enright)

Index